ON FOOT

FLORENCE WALKS

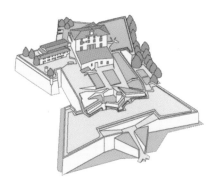

ON FOOT GUIDES

FLORENCE WALKS

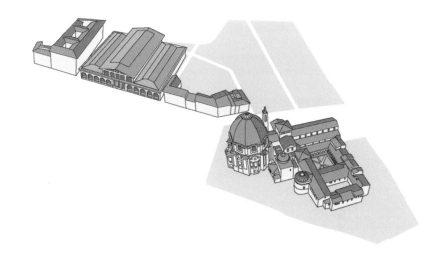

First Edition

Ella Carr

DUNCAN PETERSEN

Copyright © 2018 Duncan Petersen Publishing Ltd

This first edition conceived, designed and produced by
Duncan Petersen Publishing Limited
Studio 6, Battersea Studios
82 Silverthorne Road, London SW8 3HE
United Kingdom

Sales representation and distribution in the U.K. and Ireland by Octopus Publishing Group Ltd
Carmelite House, 20 Victoria Embankment, London, EC4Y 0DZ
Tel: 020 3122 6400

UK ISBN: 978-0-9956803-2-6

A CIP catalogue record for this book is available from the British Library.
Library of Congress Cataloging-in-Publication Data is available.

Conceived, designed and produced by
Duncan Petersen Publishing Ltd

Editorial Director Andrew Duncan

Editor Ella Carr

Maps Oxford Designers & Illustrators, Darren Lingard

Cover designed by Carl Hodson

Photographs Ella Carr

Printed by Pulsio, Bulgaria

Visit Duncan Petersen's travel website at
www.charmingsmallhotels.co.uk

CONTENTS

Exploring Florence on foot

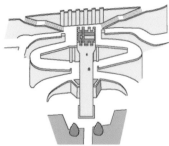

Florence is the Italian walking city *par excellence*. The unrivalled saturation of art and beauty (its entire Historic Centre is a UNESCO World Heritage Site) brings new meaning to the term 'open-air museum' – its streets and *piazzas* seethe with history. Together with its small size and idyllic situation in a valley surrounded by rolling Tuscan hills, it's little wonder the 19thC writer Henry James crowned it, "rounded pearl of cities – cheerful, compact, complete – full of a delicious mixture of beauty and convenience."

Starting out in life as an Etruscan settlement, and later the Roman colony of Florentia in 59 BC, Florence crystallized its reputation in the 15thC as the 'cradle of the Renaissance': one of the most influential artistic movements in Western history, that left behind it an awe-inspiring legacy of art, architecture and monuments. The sheer volume of artefacts in Florence means that while it is easy to explore on foot, absorbing the rich gamut the city has to offer can seem an insurmountable task.

The walks in this book are designed to help with just that. They cover the entire Historic Centre of Florence, from the districts north of the Arno to the more Bohemian neighbourhoods of Oltrarno (literally meaning the 'other side of the Arno'). A number of them take advantage of Florence's situation in the basin of a valley, taking you out to its hills and hinterlands to offer spectacular views back across the city (see **Into the Heights**, **A Hill with a View**, **Off the Beaten Track**, and **Etruscan Delights** – which explores the town of Fiesole, Florence's ancient hillside cousin, located 8km outside the city).

HOW THE MAPPING WAS MADE

A small team of specialist cartographers created the maps digitally in Adobe Illustrator. The footprint of the buildings is drawn first, then the width of the streets is artificially increased in order to give extra space for the buildings to be drawn in three dimensions. Next, the buildings are added, using aerial photography as reference. Finally the details of the buildings and the colour is added - the first very time consuming, the second less so because digital drawing programmes allow it to be automated.

Most important, the walks explore the variety of Florence. They feature all the major churches, museums and galleries, as well as a trove of lesser-known gems frequently missed by tourists, but often just as beguiling. These include a host of urban gardens, traditional food and clothing markets, and tucked-away churches and monasteries concealing sublime masterpieces (which are usually free to enter). The expertly devised twists and turns of these routes are designed to eke out the full charm of the city, and provide in-depth explorations of its neighbourhoods.

The unique aerial-view (isometric) mapping is easier to use than flat maps because you can locate yourself by the look of the buildings, as well as the street plan. The numerals on the maps are waymarks, corresponding to the directions and information about places of interest along the way. The commentaries tell the story of the city, introducing the main protagonists of its history from the Renaissance and beyond. They also set out to illuminate modern-day Florence: a bastion for *la dolce vita* and a vibrant hub in the fields of art, fashion and cookery in its own right. The **La Dolce Vita** walk (page 80) is a more wholesale celebration of Florence's cuisine and lifestyle, but all of the routes bear this theme in mind, balancing culture with more indulgent pleasures. In between churches and museums they point out the best places for *aperitivo*; the most ambient roof-top terraces for drinks, as well as the best *trattorias*, cafés, wine-bars, *gelaterias* and shops along the way. The routes also highlight many of the artisans that lace the city's cobbled streets, representing yet another lively vein of history still pumping through present-day Florence. Their hand-crafted designs are considered among the best in the world.

Henry James might have likened Florence to a pearl, but for the tourist the city presents itself as a multi-faceted diamond – one that deserves to be appreciated from all angles, whether this be plonked in front of Michelangelo's *David*, or settling into *piazza*-life with an *aperol spritz* in hand. If you complete all 12 walks you can claim to know Florence very well indeed, and will have mastered the Florentine art of living along the way.

Master Map

1. The Birth of the Renaissance 20-29
2. Power & Patronage 30-39
3. Walking with Ghosts 40-49
4. Sacred Spaces 50-59
5. Living it up with the Locals 60-69
6. The Boboli Gardens 70-79
7. La Dolce Vita 80-87
8. Into the Heights 88-95
9. Off the Beaten Track 96-101
10. A Hill with a View 102-109
11. Last Supper Trail 110-119
12. Etruscan Delights (bus caught here) 120-127

Mercato Centrale

Via Nazionale

Via dell'Ariento

Firenze SMN Stazione

Piazza della Stazione

Largo Fratelli Alinari

Via S Antonio

S Maria Novella

S Lorenzo

Via Palazzuolo

Via della Scala

Piazza S Maria Novella

Via degli Antinori

Via delle belle Donne

S Gaetano

Via dei Vecchietti

Ognissanti

Via del Porcellana

Piazza Ognissanti

Via dei Fossi

Via Tornabuoni

Via dei Pescioni

Piazza di Repubbl

Via Orsan-michele

Borgo S Frediano

Ponte alla Carraia

S Trinita

Via Porta Rossa

Mer Vec

S Frediano in Cestello

Via del'Orto

Via S Spirito

Ponte S Trinita

Piazza Carmine

Via della Chiesa

S Maria del Carmine

Via S Agostino

S Spirito

Piazza de' Frescobaldi

Ponte Vecchio

Piazza Torquato Tasso

Via del Campuccio

Via dei Serragli

Via del Caldai

Via del Presto di S Martino

Via de Guicciardini

S Felicita

Via Maggio

Piazza de' Pitti

Palazzo Pitti

del Casone

Via Roma

Via Fracesco Petrarca

Giardino Boboli

Forte Belve

Porta Romana
10

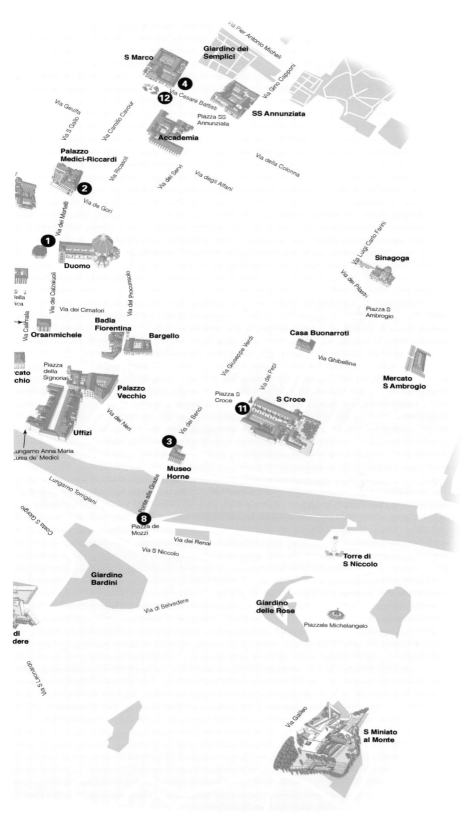

HOW TO USE THIS BOOK

Exploring both sides of the Arno, the walks cover the entire Historic Centre of Florence, from Piazza della Liberta in the north to Porta Romana in the south, and from Porta di San Frediano in the west to Porta alla Croce in the east. A few of the walks go beyond the Historic Centre (which is loosely bounded by the 14thC city walls and their ancient Portas): **A Hill with A View** winds up to the rural hill top of Bellosguardo; **Into the Heights** extends beyond Porta San Niccolò to the hill top monastery of San Miniato al Monte; **Off the Beaten Track** heads towards the suburb of Arcetri before tracing the city walls to Porta San Miniato; and **Etruscan Delights** is based in Fiesole, 3km outside of Florence.

Using the maps

The route of each walk is clearly marked on the map, with the occasional arrow to keep you heading in the right direction. This guide indicates where the walk starts and finishes, as well as the nearest bus stop where necessary (though because of Florence's small size, walking is often the most expedient means of travel).

Numerals on the maps correspond to the numerals in the text, marking the start of each section of the walk. Street names are shown in bold print, as are places of interest such as buildings, museums, galleries, restaurants, cafés, or shops.

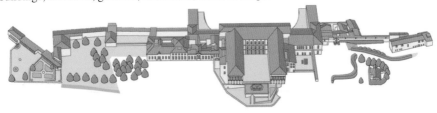

LINKING THE WALKS

The compactness of the city centre combined with its high concentration of things to see means several of the walks run close to each other, or even cross over at points. If you have the energy to complete one walk and then move on to another, or interweave parts of two walks, there are various interesting combinations. The four walks north of the Arno – **The Birth of the Renaissance**, **Walking With Ghosts**, **Sacred Spaces** and **Power and Patronage** – are all in close proximity, their respective start and end points rarely being more than a ten-minute walk from each other. They complement each other in their focus on galleries, museums and churches, though for this same reason it might be advisable to spread them out across your trip, for fear of risking cultural indigestion. **Last Supper Trail** travels in an arc across the same area as these walks, so the *cenacoli* could be integrated into the four walks rather than visited in one go. **Into the Heights** and **Off the Beaten Track** both explore the hilly area to the east of Oltrarno, and share the same end point, so could easily be merged by doing one in reverse. The start and end points of the other Oltrarno walks, **Living it up with the Locals**, **A Bucolic Ramble** and **A Hill with a View**, are all less than ten minutes from each other, so a morning spent on one could easily bleed into an afternoon spent on another. **La Dolce Vita** covers much of the same ground as **Living it up with the Locals** with added emphasis on food and drink, so the two could be merged for a *tour de force* of the Oltrarno area that combines culture, shopping, food, and a healthy dose of day-drinking.

WHEN TO USE THIS BOOK

Most of the walks can be enjoyed throughout the year, but a few factors – such as weather and crowd-intensity levels – make certain walks more suited to particular seasons.

Spring/Summer walks

• **The Boboli Gardens**: these stay open all year round but come into their full and fragrant glory during the summer months. They also provide much needed respite from the heat, with plenty of shaded areas to sunbathe on the cool grass.
• **Etruscan Delights**: the town of Fiesole is beautiful at any time of year, but the swathes of Tuscan countryside around it look their loveliest in summer. The town is also a bit livelier at this time of year, when a number of Florentines arrive to escape the sticky heat of the city, and open-air concerts are held in Fiesole's ancient Roman *anfiteatro*.
• **Into the Heights**: the hill top monastery of San Miniato al Monte is always worth a trip, but the Giardino delle Rose en route is at its most radiant in spring/summer – particularly between May and June when all 350 species of rose are in bloom. This also applies to **Off the Beaten Track**, which runs via the Giardino Bardini. For both these walks, the warmer months are amenable to *al fresco* drinks at wine bars along the way, and the views across Florence will be enhanced by the bright summer sun. The same might be said for **A Hill with a View**, which offers one of the best vistas over Florence.
• **La Dolce Vita**: the 'party walk', which celebrates the food and nightlife of Florence, is best saved for spring/summer when a special kind of festival buzz descends upon the city. This does not necessarily include the month of August, when a large portion of Florentines evacuate the city.

Autumn/Winter walks

• From June until August the crowds of tourists begin to flood in the city, significantly enlarging the queues to its most

famous attractions. The heat and humidity of these months mean standing in long queues and consuming culture can be physically draining. Art-enthusiasts – particularly first-time visitors wishing to tick off the major attractions, such as climbing the dome of the cathedral, and visiting the Uffizi and Accademia galleries – might wish to visit outside of these months. The walks this applies to most are **The Birth of the Renaissance**, **Walking With Ghosts**, **Power & Patronage**, **Sacred Spaces** and **Last Supper Trail**, which encompass many of the more mainstream attractions. They're especially heavy on indoor attractions such as galleries, churches and museums, making them useful for cold and rainy days. **Walking With Ghosts** is especially charming at Christmas when the Piazza di Santa Croce holds its annual German Christmas Market (the same *piazza* should be avoided in June when it hosts Calcio Storico, the violent football tournament held between the city's historic neighbourhoods).

WEEKEND WALKS

• **Etruscan Delights:** the quiet town of Fiesole becomes livelier on weekends. A buzzing market is held in its Piazza Mino every Saturday, with a fantastic antiques market held every first Saturday and Sunday of the month.

• **La Dolce Vita:** during the *fiesta* summer season Florence is buzzing any night of the week, but this is predictably amplified on weekends, when *piazzas* swell with bonhomie until the late/early hours.

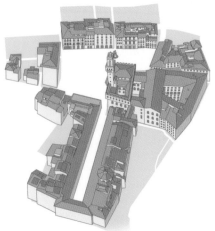

WEEKDAY WALKS

Planning around the capricious opening hours of museums, churches and shops in Florence can be a challenge – one that is sometimes best attempted on weekdays (though most Italian state museums, such as the Uffizi and Accademia, are shut on Mondays). The opening hours for churches are often subject to change, so it's always worth double-checking the opening times below before setting off.

• **Living it up with the Locals**: the typical schedule for Oltrarno artisans that feature heavily on this walk is between Monday and Friday during the hours 9.30am-12.30pm and 3.30pm-7.30pm (shutting for *siesta* time). They're less reliable on weekends, sometimes only open by appointment. Their schedule is roughly reflected in that of churches on this route. For example, the Basilica di Santo Spirito, which is closed on weekends and Wednesdays, is otherwise open between 9.30am-12.30pm and 4pm-5.30pm.

• **Last Supper Trail:** timing this walk to the opening hours of the *cenacoli* can be tricky. Cenacolo Foligno opens on Tuesdays and Wednesdays; Cenacolo di Ognissanti on Mondays, Tuesdays and Saturdays; San Salvi between Tuesday – Saturday. This means the golden window for completing this walk is on a Tuesday. However, the route overlaps with a number of the other walks, so you needn't do it all in one go.

• **Power and Patronage:** the Basilica di Santa Trinita at the end of this walk is only open on weekdays, between 8am-12pm and 4pm-6pm. The Chiesa di Ognissanti is open daily between 9.30am-12.30pm and 4pm-7.30pm, but is shut Wednesday mornings, whilst its *cenacolo* is only open on Mondays, Tuesdays and Saturdays until 12pm. The larger churches on this walk open daily, without a *siesta* break.

• **Sacred Spaces:** the Chiostro dello Scalzo is only open on Mondays and Thursdays (as well as the 1st, 3rd and 5th Saturday of the month), while the Galleria dell'Accademia is shut on Mondays – so if at all possible, complete this walk on a Thursday.

WALKS FOR KIDS

Florence is not easy for kids – the sheer concentration of galleries, museums and churches can make it a toddler's nightmare. While all of the walks weave in pit-stops of *gelato* and cafés, a couple of them are more enjoyable for little people.

• **The Boboli Gardens**: these are hugely popular with Florentine families on weekends because they're perfect for children. The rolling green spaces are made for running, playing and picnicking, while their inherent wackiness – grottoes dripping in stalactites, and mythical statues emerging from every hedge – appeal to a nipper's imagination.

• **Living it up with the Locals**: this explores the less hectic Oltrarno side of the river, with added emphasis on food stops – including *gelato* and pastries to keep little ones happy. There's still a couple of churches along the way, but minimum queues and crowding, as well as a number of artisan craft shops to buy souvenirs from.

• **Into the Heights**: the way up to San Miniato al Monte can be a fun excursion for kids. They can be set free to roam in the Giardino delle Rose – with its quirky hybrid-animal sculptures by Jean-Michel Folon concealed in the shrubbery – and can use the free binoculars on Piazzale Michelangelo to look out across the whole of Florence. San Miniato monastery's cemetery with its elaborate tombstones holds a morbid fascination for children, and there's a gift shop selling ice cream and cake. If they get tired you can bypass the return route, and catch the No. 12 bus from outside San Miniato al Monte on Via Galileo, to get back to the centre.

GETTING TO FLORENCE

You can fly directly to Firenze Airport. From here it's a half-hour bus journey or a 15 minute taxi transfer to the centre. It's reasonably well served by budget airlines such as Vueling and British Airways, but another popular option is flying to Pisa. This is a slightly larger airport, with a wider selection of airlines such as Ryanair, and therefore often cheaper. From Pisa you can either catch one of the buses that leave every few minutes outside of the airport, taking just over an hour, or catch the eight minute

Pisa Mover connecting the airport to Pisa Centrale station, and then a train to Florence, taking just under an hour. Both bus and train come to about the same price, and disembark at Santa Maria Novella station in the centre of Florence.

GETTING AROUND

By far the best way to get around Florence is on foot. The Historic Centre of Florence (spanning both sides of the river) covers a mere 505 hectares, and can be walked from one end to the other in just over 30 minutes. For this reason Florence does not have a metro system, though it does have a bus network and a (limited) tram line. Where relevant the walks in this book include information on catching buses back to the centre, but more often than not the start/end points of the routes fall within the Historic Centre, making it more convenient to walk to your next destination.

Buses and trams
Florence has two major bus lines. 'Le City Line di Firenze' has a small network of four routes covering the area immediately around the Historic Centre. However, Florence is full of cobbled streets and alleyways too narrow for buses to pass through, so these lines have limited access to the sights. Since the Duomo was pedestrianised, the majority of these buses can be picked up outside Santa Maria Novella Station, or Piazza San Marco. 'ATAF' and 'LI-NEA' – the suburban bus services leading out of the city – also leave from these two bus hubs.

Since 2010 there's also been the T1 tramline that runs from Scandicci to Santa Maria Novella station. As we went to press two additional tram lines were being built – one from Firenze Airport and another from

FLORENCE

EMERGENCY INFORMATION

Emergency Police: 113
Carabinieri: 112
Fire Department: 115
Road Assistance: 116
Ambulance: 118

If you need to report a theft/loss, you can find English language assistance at the following police stations:
Polizia, Via Pietrapiana, 50r. Questura, Via Zara, 2.
Carabinieri, Borgo Ognissanti, 48.

Hospitals with 24-hour emergency departments and English speaking doctors:
Ospedale S. Maria Nuova, Piazza S. Maria Nuova, 1. Tel: 055-69381.
Ospedale Pediatrico A.Meyer (Children's Hospital), Viale Pieraccini 24. Tel: 055-56621.
Ospedale di Careggi, Largo Brambilla, 3. Foreign Patients: 055-794-7057 or 055-794-9888.
Nuovo Ospedale di San Giovanni di Dio a Torregalli, Via Torre Galli, 3. Tel: 055-69321.

The Farmacia Comunale in Santa Maria Novella Station is 24-hour, usually with at least one English speaking member of staff. Tel. 055-289435.

Careggi hospital, both leading downtown to the centre.

Tickets

It's important to buy tickets *before* getting on the bus, as the driver lets everyone on without checking them, and the fine for not having one if one of the many inspectors gets on board is substantial. Once on the bus, put your ticket in the 'ticket validating machine', which will print the time and date on the ticket. You then have 90 minutes to complete the journey – meaning you can get on and off other buses within that time frame using the same ticket. There's an ATAF ticket booth in Piazza della Stazione (on your left as you leave the station). Tickets can also be purchased at various sales points around the city (cafés, tobacconists etc) that have ATAF stickers on their shop windows. As we went to press, one 90 minute ticket cost €1.20; you could also buy a 24-hour ticket for €5, and a 3-day ticket for €12.

ATAF tickets are also valid on the city's tram lines, likewise to be purchased before getting on the tram.

Taxis

Taxis cannot be flagged down in Florence, but instead are stationed at various taxi stands around the city, or you can telephone the following taxi numbers for a pick up: 055-4242 / 055-4390 / 055-4798 / 055-4499. As we went to press the set fare for Florence Airport to/from the centre was €22 (€25 at night) with a €1 charge for baggage. Bear in mind there's a minimum charge of €5 when travelling anywhere in the centre. Otherwise, take the fare from the meter, rounding it up to the nearest euro.

Bicycles

A number of Florentines use bicycles as their primary means of getting around, but as in any busy city it's important to be vigilant of motorists and pedestrians. Getting around the Historic Centre on bicycle can be very practical, as many areas are closed off to motor traffic, but it can also be more congested and lacking in bike lanes. There are a number of bike rental services in Florence, one of the cheapest being Ulysses (www.cooperativaulisse.it). These purple bikes can be picked up near the taxi stand outside Santa Maria Novella Station. Their rates as we went to press were: one hour = €2; five hours = €5; one day = €10.

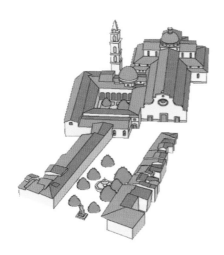

TOURIST INFORMATION

Florence is well served by tourist information offices and websites – at each one you can get up-to-date timetables of all the museums, daily events, and where to find accommodation if you haven't already. The info points for the official tourist website of the Metropolitan City of Florence (www.firenzeturismo.it) are at the following addresses:
• Piazza del Duomo (main tourist office).
• Piazza della Stazione, 4.
• Via Camillo Cavour, 1r (specializing in the six areas of Florentine territory besides the city itself, including Fiesole and Chianti). The websites Visit Florence (www.visitflorence.com) and The Museums of Florence (www.museumsinflorence.com) also provide a variety of helpful insider information.

Travelling with children

For information on events (often held around the city's museums) and special family tours, visit www.firenzeturismo.it, and head to the category 'Families & kids.'

Disabled travellers

Florence's cobbled streets and crowded pavements can present challenges to the disabled tourist. While ATAF buses have disabled access, there are no buses connecting the Duomo, Accademia, Uffizi and Ponte Vecchio. Fortunately they're bunched close together, but this still requires navigating several blocks of cobblestones and crowd congestion.

However, its smallness and high concentration of sights at the centre means Florence is in many ways suited to disabled visitors, for despite being set in a basin the centre of the city is predominantly flat. Wheelchair accommodation is cheaper than in Rome or Venice, and several of the attractions are free for disabled tourists, including the Accademia and Uffizi galleries. For more guidance on disabled access in Florence visit www.firenzeturismo.it and click on the category 'Florence without barriers.'

Bus tours

A bus tour can give you a useful overview of the city, despite the areas between the Duomo and Ponte Vecchio being pedestrianized. The Hop-on/Hop-off open top bus departs every 30 minutes from Piazza Stazione SMN, ending up at Barbetti. The tour takes about an hour, following 16km route around the city that covers many of its major landmarks.

Museum entry

Florence is invariably crowded, especially in the summer months when you can expect long queues snaking towards the main attractions. During this period a FirenzeCard can be useful for streamlining your visit. It costs €72 and is valid for 72 hours, giving you admission to 72 museums, villas and historical gardens located in and around Florence. It also provides unlimited travel on ATAF/LI-NEA bus and tram lines (which you won't need to use while exploring the centre), free wi-fi around the city – and, perhaps most usefully, it permits priority access to the sights, so you can skip queues without making a reservation (with the exception of the Cupola). The FirenzeCard is worth keeping in mind if you're visiting in peak season for a limited amount of time – depending on how many sights you wish to cram into 72 hours.

Opening hours

State-run museums and galleries, such as the Uffizi, Accademia and Palatine Gallery, are always closed on Mondays. Others have alternate closing days across the month (e.g. they might be open the 1st and 3rd Sunday of the month, but closed on the 2nd and 4th) so it's always worth checking online beforehand. Major museums are usually open between 8.15am and 6.30pm.

The bigger churches, such as Santa Maria Novella and Santa Croce, keep similar museum hours between 9.30am to 5.30pm, while the smaller (usually free) churches are generally open between 9.30am – noon, and again between 3.30 – 5.30pm, notwithstanding closures on specific days, which we've tried to include in this guide but it is nonetheless advisable to check beforehand, as they are subject to change (the same goes for *cenacoli* and monasteries).

Shopping and banking hours

Many of the bigger shops and chain stores in the heart of Florence have taken on a full working day, opening between 10am and 7pm. However, a number of the smaller shops, as well as boutique stores and artisans, open between between 9am – 12.30pm and 3.30 – 7pm, and close Sundays. A number of the traditional artisans are only open on weekends by appointment.

Banks generally remain open between Monday and Friday, from 8.30am to 13.30pm, and again between 3pm and 4pm (though times vary between them, and some are open on Saturday mornings). Restaurants open between 12pm – 2.30pm and 7pm –

11pm, with a few closing on Sundays.

Public holidays

- 1 January (New Year's Day)
- 6 January (Epiphany)
- Easter Sunday
- Easter Monday
- 25 April (Liberation Day)
- 1 May (Labour Day)
- 2 June (Anniversary of the Republic)
- 15 August (Assumption of the Virgin)
- 1 November (All Saints' Day)
- 8 December (Day of the Immaculate Conception)
- 25 December (Christmas Day)
- 26 December (Boxing Day – known in Italy as *Santo Stefano*)

TIPPING

Service is usually included in the price (look for *servizio* on the bill), but it is customary to leave something on the table after you have paid your bill if you are particularly pleased with the service. If your restaurant bill does not include service, add 10-15 per cent. In cafés and bars, tips are not expected although it is usual to leave a few coins. It is always less expensive to stand at a bar to consume your drink or snack than sit at a table. Pay first and give the receipt to the barman with your order.

Introducing Florence on Foot

This itinerary is designed to give an introduction to Florence. It's longer than the other walks in the guide, but very useful to anyone with only a day to explore. It takes in most of the key sights and will give you an idea of what Florence is about, without exploring it in depth. Mainly sticking to the major thoroughfares, the route introduces you to some of the famous landmarks, helping you find your bearings, both north and south of the Arno. Depending on how long you linger at each sight, the route could take up the best part of a day.

Begin at **Firenze Santa Maria Novella** railway station – a central location and the logical starting point for those arriving to the city by rail or bus. Standing in its *piazza*, with the back of the **Basilica di Santa Maria Novella** straight ahead of you on the opposite side, bear left down **Largo Fratelli Alinari**, which quickly turns into **Via Nazionale**. Take the second right down **Via dell'Ariento**, which hosts the lively street market of San Lorenzo neighbourhood – *the* place for souvenirs and knock-off designer goods. The **Mercato Centrale** will loom on your left (see **Power & Patronage**, page 34), the epicentre of the city's food artisans and an ideal breakfast stop-off, before continuing down **Via dell'Ariento**.

When you arrive into **Piazza di San Lorenzo** walk down the side of **Basilica di San Lorenzo** until its unfinished façade emerges on your right. This – the oldest and largest basilica in the city – was the local church of the ruling Medici family, and burial place of its principal members (see **Power & Patronage**, page 33). At the end of the *piazza* turn left down **Via de'Ginori**, and you'll find their historic residence, the **Palazzo Medici Riccardi**, at its corner on your right (see **Power & Patronage**, page 32). Its courtyards and sculpture displays are free to the public, while tickets can be bought to see its luscious apartments and the **Magi Chapel**.

Emerge from the other side on to **Via Camillo Cavour** and turn right, keeping straight as the street merges on to **Via de'Martelli**. Continue until you arrive into **Piazza del Duomo**, with its famous triumvirate of architectural monuments: **Giotto's bell tower**; the **Baptistery**, with its two sets of bronze doors cast by Lorenzo Ghiberti in the 15thC, and accredited with kick-starting the Renaissance; and the **Cattedrale di Santa Maria del Fiore**, surmounted by Brunelleschi's iconic dome (see **The Birth of the Renaissance**, page 22-23). After exploring the *piazza*, head to its far corner at the Baptistery end, and turn left down **Via Roma**. This takes you into **Piazza della Repubblica**, a major *piazza* and the original site of the Roman forum when Florence was founded as a Roman colony in 59 BC.

Continue in the same direction out of the *piazza* down **Via Calimala**, and take the first right down **Via Orsanmichele**. **Chiesa di Orsanmichele** will appear at the second block on your right, a former grain market turned church, with outside niches populated by Renaissance sculptures commissioned by trade guilds during the Renaissance (see **Centro Storico**, page 24).

Turn right down **Via dei Calzaiuoli** and continue until you arrive in **Piazza della Signoria**, the civic heart of Florence and seat of the **Palazzo Vecchio** – a medieval fortress, built on the ruins of an ancient Roman *anfiteatro*. Have a drink at the historic **Caffè Rivoire**, and a gander among the *piazza's* many sculptures, before heading into **Piazzale degli Uffizi**

FLORENCE

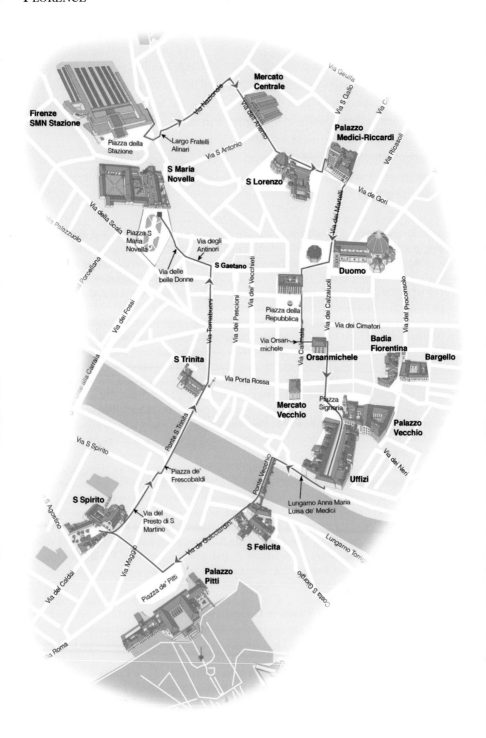

at the corner of **Palazzo Vecchio** and the **Loggia dei Lanzi**. Walk to the end of the Piazzale – seat of Florence's most famous gallery, the **Uffizi** (see **Centro Storico**, page 26). Exit through the arch at the end and turn right down **Lungarno Anna Maria Luisa de' Medici**, walking along the side of the Arno.

Cross the **Ponte Vecchio** – Florence's oldest surviving bridge and seat of the city's gold merchants – which will take you to the historic artisan district of Oltrarno. Once off the bridge go straight down **Via de'Guicciardini** (dipping into **Basilica Santa Felicita** in **Piazza Santa Felicita** if you wish to see Jacopo Pontormo's masterpiece, *The Deposition*) (see **Living it up with the Locals**, page 62). **Via de'Guicciardini** takes you into **Piazza de' Pitti**, with the vast **Palazzo Pitti** on your left – easily the grandest *palazzo* in Florence, and home to a number of impressive art collections, while the *piazza* itself is lined with cafés, wine bars and artisans. (see **Living it up with the Locals**, page 63-64).

Take a right down **Sdrucciolo de'Pitti**, a narrow cobbled street lined with yet more artisans, and continue in same direction as it merges on to **Via de' Michelozzi**, arriving into **Piazza Santo Spirito** (see **Living it up with the Locals,** page 65). The beating heart of Oltrarno, this *piazza* is often populated with market stalls by day, and filled with partying revellers by night. Its myriad cafés and restaurants make it the perfect lunch spot (**Osteria di Santo Spirito** being the best). Pop into the **Basilica di Santo Spirito** with an interior designed by Brunelleschi, before leaving the *piazza* down **Via del Presto di S. Martino** (walking down the side of the basilica). Turn right at **Borgo S. Jacopo**, then take an immediate left into **Piazza de' Frescobaldi**. Buy an ice cream at **Gelateria Santa Trinita** (best flavour: Black Sesame) before crossing **Ponte Santa Trinita** – another of the city's historic bridges, proffering the best view of its neighbouring Ponte Vecchio.

Once off the bridge keep straight down **Via Tornabuoni**, a major thoroughfare lined with *palazzi* and designer stores. The **Basilica di Santa Trinita** will appear soon on your left – another free church with a famous fresco cycle by Ghirlandaio (see **Power & Patronage**, page 39). Further along is the monumental **Palazzo Strozzi**, which frequently holds exhbitions, and at **no. 65** is **Procacci**, an atmospheric wine bar that's been open since 1885. Continue down this street until you arrive at **Chiesa dei Santi Michele e Gaetano** in **Piazza degli Antinori** – yet another free church, with a stunning interior. From here go left down **Via degli Antinori**, then right down **Via delle Belle Donne**. Continue to the end of this road, turning left at **Via dei Banchi**, which takes you to your final stop in **Piazza di Santa Maria Novella**. The *piazza* is the seat of **Basilica di Santa Maria Novella**, with its iconic polychrome façade designed by Alberti (see **Power & Patronage**, page 34). Inside, the church brims with artworks, including Masaccio's seminal *Trinity*.

If you're leaving Florence by railway or bus, walk down **Via degli Avelli** along the side of the basilica, which takes you back into **Piazza della Stazione**. If you're staying in the centre, it will likely be a short walk or taxi drive home (closest taxi rank outside SMN station).

The Birth of the Renaissance: Centro Storico

I t is at the starting point of this walk, wedged between Florence's Baptistery and Cathedral, that the story of the Italian – and European – Renaissance began to unfold. A competition held in 1401 to discover a sculptor to design a new set of bronze doors for the Baptistery is famously seen to have heralded the beginning of a movement that would illuminate the following two centuries across Europe. Lorenzo Ghiberti was chosen as the competition's victor, and spent the following 50 years casting two sets of doors. His competitor – the famously irascible and arrogant Brunelleschi – was so enraged by this snub that he forsook sculpture altogether, becoming instead Florence's leading architect. The fruits of his wounded pride can be seen in *palazzi* and churches throughout the city, but most impressively across the square in the form of his formidable dome – an architectural feat so astounding it has become an emblem for the achievements of the Florentine Renaissance.

This circuit takes you through the city's densely packed historic centre, making it an ideal introductory walk to the city, acquainting you with the history of Florence as well as a number of her most iconic landmarks – which will serve as major reference points during your stay.

The Gates of Paradise,
cast by Lorenzo Ghiberti.

Perseus with the Head of Medusa,
by Benvenuto Cellini (1554), in
the Loggia dei Lanzi.

▶ **STARTS**
The Baptistery, in Piazza del Duomo.

■ **ENDS**
Piazza del Duomo.

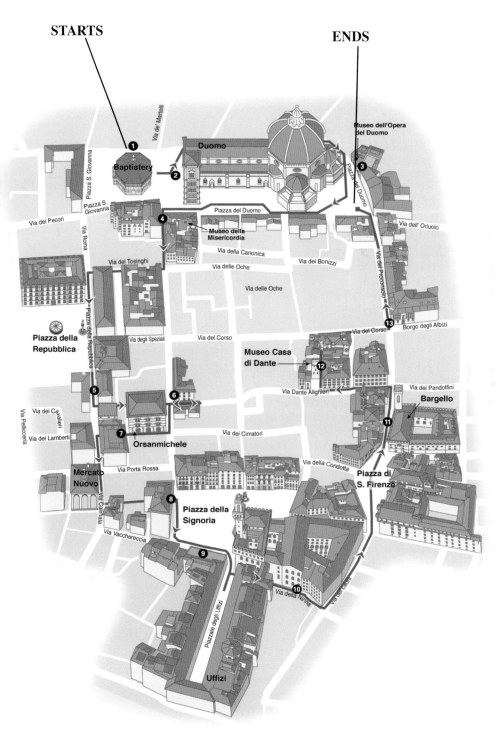

STARTS

ENDS

21

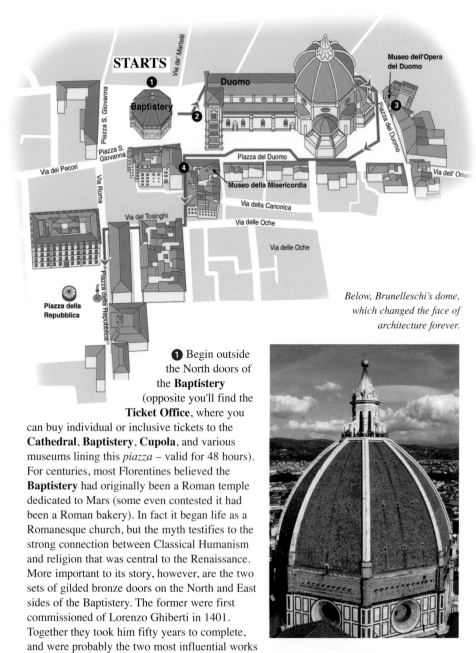

STARTS

Museo dell'Opera del Duomo

Duomo

Baptistery

Via de' Martelli

Piazza S. Giovanna

Piazza del Duomo

Piazza del Duomo

Via dei Pecori

Piazza S. Giovanna

Via Roma

Museo della Misericordia

Via dell' Oriuo

Via della Canonica

Via del Tosinghi

Via delle Oche

Via delle Oche

Piazza della Repubblica

Piazza della Repubblica

Below, Brunelleschi's dome, which changed the face of architecture forever.

❶ Begin outside the North doors of the **Baptistery** (opposite you'll find the **Ticket Office**, where you can buy individual or inclusive tickets to the **Cathedral**, **Baptistery**, **Cupola**, and various museums lining this *piazza* – valid for 48 hours). For centuries, most Florentines believed the **Baptistery** had originally been a Roman temple dedicated to Mars (some even contested it had been a Roman bakery). In fact it began life as a Romanesque church, but the myth testifies to the strong connection between Classical Humanism and religion that was central to the Renaissance. More important to its story, however, are the two sets of gilded bronze doors on the North and East sides of the Baptistery. The former were first commissioned of Lorenzo Ghiberti in 1401. Together they took him fifty years to complete, and were probably the two most influential works of art in that century. Take a close look at the panels on *The Gates of Paradise* on the East Side (the later and more resplendent of the two). Ghiberti's use of perspective, Classical architecture and realism give you a sense of the new priorities of Renaissance art, largely inspired by a renewed interest in Classical antiquity.

Panel on the North Doors:
The Annunciation.

Panel on the East Doors:
Joseph Sold into Slavery.

2 Opposite *The Gates of Paradise*, the **Duomo's** façade looms before you – a smorgasbord of marble inlay, stained-glass, mosaics and sculptures – flanked by Giotto's *campanile* (bell tower) on the right. In the 13thC a slew of churches were commissioned by the Florentine Republic, including Santa Croce, Santa Maria Novella, and, most eminently, the Duomo, to reflect the growing prosperity of Florence. Walk the entire diameter to appreciate its staggering proportions, inlaid with white Carrara, green Prato and red Marenna marbles – and of course to admire

Decorative head on the North Door.

Brunelleschi's dome (which is perhaps best appreciated from afar). In 1418 few believed the crowning of a dome 138 feet in diameter even possible, but Brunelleschi ingeniously managed it by designing a double-layered dome, reinforced by bricks laid out in a herringbone pattern. If you have a ticket, and don't mind heights, climb to the base of the dome for the best viewpoint of the inside of the church – but in the summer be prepared for queues snaking down the length of the Cathedral.

3 At the dome end of the *piazza* is the **Museo dell'Opera Duomo**. Founded in 1296 to oversee the building of the Cathedral, it's since served as a conservatory for artworks from the Duomo and Baptistery. Here you can find the original bronze doors protected from the elements, alongside a spell-binding collection of monuments.

4 Once you've circuited the Cathedral, take a left down **Via dei Calzaiuoli**. Go right again down **Via dei Tosinghi** (unless you want to make a quick detour to **GROM**, the renowned *gelateria*, in which case take the first left down **Via delle Oche** to **no. 24**). Then take the first left down **Via Roma**, which brings you into **Piazza della Repubblica**. During the city's Roman infancy this marked the site of its central Forum. Its current Neoclassical garb dates to the brief 19thC interim in which Florence was made capital of Italy. Its **Caffè Paszkowski (no. 35/r)** began as a Polish brewery in the 19thC Jewish ghetto, before it moved to this prestigious site and became a hangout for artists. Now slightly overpriced, it clings to the glory of its bohemian past, but holds charming open-air concerts in the summer.

5 Go down **Via Calimala**, taking the first left along **Via dei Orsanmichele**, and the **Chiesa di Orsanmichele** (open 10am-5pm every day) will come up on your right. Built as a grain market in 1290, it became a church after it acquired a miraculous image of the Virgin Mary. In 1404 each of its exterior niches were allocated to one of the major guilds. The guilds played a huge role in the running the Republic of Florence, and their patronage fuelled the city's art and architecture during the Renaissance. Orsanmichele was seen as an opportunity for them to engage in friendly (or not-so-friendly) rivalry, by appointing the best artists in the city to fill the niches. Perhaps the most famous sculpture appears very soon on your right: Donatello's *St George* – a masterpiece

Donatello's St George.

of psychological realism, in which St George leans on his shield and stares stoically into the distance, having just vanquished the dragon. The story is told in the *rilievo schiacciato* (scratched relief) panel, underneath the statue. Donatello designed the sculpture to be seen from directly below, so if you cross the road to look at St George his head becomes disproportionately small – a typically Renaissance illusionist trick.

6 Dip into **Via dei Cimatori** to reach **Due Fratellini**, three shops down to your left. A traditional Italian hole-in-the-wall, this is a delectable spot to grab a sandwich (go for one of their *tartufo* options) and a glass of *rosso* before continuing on your walk around the length of the church – taking in its niche sculptures as you go. Other notable ones include *Christ & St Thomas* by Andrea del Verocchio, and *St Mark* by Donatello.

Orsanmichele.

Il Porcellino.

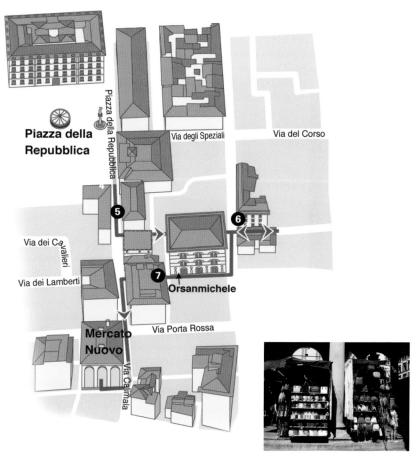

Mercato Nuovo.

❼ Head down **Via dei Lamberti**, turning left to rejoin **Via Calimala**. Straight ahead you will see the vaulted arches of the **Mercato Nuovo**, deceptively named since it's been around since the time of Dante, when cloth merchants sold their wares alongside apothecaries, prostitutes and shouting salesman (now it specializes in leather and souvenirs). Walk to the centre of the loggia and you'll find a stone that looks like a wheel embedded in the floor. So-called the *pietra dell'acculata* (literally meaning 'stone of the butt') because of the part it played in the unorthodox punishment of dishonest merchants 500 years ago, who were stripped naked with their hands and feet tied, and dropped bare-bottomed on the stone three times before having their possessions divided. This is the origin of the common Florentine saying *stare culo a terra* – 'to have ones butt on the ground' – meaning to be broke. Before leaving the market be sure to rub the nose of *Il Porcellino*, to ensure your return to Florence (as the superstition goes).

❽ Head down **Via Calimaruzza**, which will take you into **Piazza della Signoria**. This square has long been the centre of Florentine political and ceremonial life, bearing witness to the city's most turbulent phases of history. It was here, for example, that the fanatical Dominican monk Savonarola

Palazzo Vecchio.

(who briefly ousted the Medici in 1494) held his Bonfires of Vanities, only to be burned at the stake on the same spot seven years later. Today the square serves as a sort of open-air museum. The **Palazzo Vecchio** is guarded by a number of sculptures, including Donatello's *Marzocco* (lion), a copy of his *Judith & Holofernes* and of Michelangelo's *David*. All three are potent symbols of the Republic: suitable mascots for a building that has been at the centre of civic life since the 13thC (and boasts the tallest tower in the city). While still used as a town hall, its frescoed apartments are open to the public (Mon-Wed, Sat-Sun).

❾ The **Loggia dei Lanzi** shelters an array of phenomenal Mannerist sculptures. Giambologna's *Rape of the Sabine Women* (1583) is especially captivating: its spiralling composition is designed to be viewed 'in the round', making it powerful from any viewpoint. Have a *caffè* outside the famous **Caffè Rivoire** before leaving the *piazza* at the corner of the **Palazzo Vecchio** and the **Loggia dei Lanzi**, to reach **Piazzale degli Uffizi**, the seat of the **Uffizi Gallery**. Without a doubt one of the finest in the world, its overwhelming collection includes masterpieces such as Boticelli's *Birth of Venus* and Titian's *Venus of Urbino*. Avoid the sometimes mammoth queues by booking in advance.

The Rape of the
Sabine Women
by Giambologna.

The Marzocco *(a traditional symbol of Florence), by Flaminio Vacca.*

The Birth of Venus *by Boticelli.*

➓ Walk down **Via della Ninna**, down the side of the **Palazzo Vecchio**, and take the first left down **Via dei Leoni**. This takes you to **Piazza di San Firenze**, with the **Complesso di San Firenzo** on your right, garnished with frothy Baroque sculptures. Continue straight across the square down **Via Proconsolo**, approaching the **Bargello** on your right. This fortified tower has had a number of incarnations across Florentine history: first built by the Guelph government in 1250 under the title of *Palazzo Popolo*, it then became a prison and torture chamber in the 14thC and 15thC, when the bodies of executed criminals were customarily displayed in its courtyard (Savonarola was tortured in one of its cells before being dragged to his gruesome end in the Piazza della Signoria). The Medici also made it the headquarters of the chief of police, hence its current sobriquet *bargello*. Now, however, this austere setting houses one of Florence's most prestigious sculpture collections, including Donatello's wonderfully effete bronze *David* – a dramatic contrast to Michelangelo's stoic rendition of the city's favourite hero, in the Accademia.

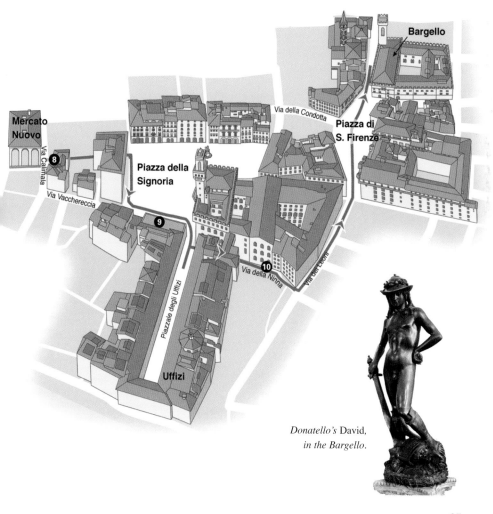

Donatello's David,
in the Bargello.

27

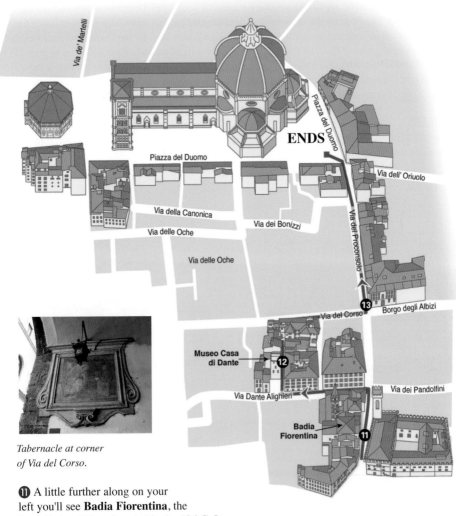

*Tabernacle at corner
of Via del Corso.*

⓫ A little further along on your
left you'll see **Badia Fiorentina**, the
Benedictine Abbey founded in the 10thC. It
has been rebuilt many times since, but retains its
Romanesque *campanile* and wooden coffered ceiling.
It contains Filippo Lippi's 1486 altarpiece of *The Virgin Appearing to St Bernard*. Take the
left turn just past it, down **Via Dante Alighieri**, and you will have officially entered
medieval Florence: the streets in this central pocket haven't changed for at least 700 years.
Keep following this road and you enter into a small courtyard, with the **Museo Casa di
Dante** straight ahead (open 10am-6pm every day). The museum is dedicated to the poet and
father of the Italian language, who was born on this spot in 1265 – where he most likely
remained until he was exiled from Florence in 1302.

⓬ Head down **Via Santa Margherita** and you will soon find the tiny **Santa Maria dei Cerchi**, more commonly known as **Chiesa di Dante** because of the role it plays in Dante's life story. It was here, at the tender age of nine, the poet supposedly first clapped eyes on his true love Beatrice Portinari (whose family tombs were placed here), and where he later married Gemma Donati. It still contains a rather lovely *Madonna Enthroned* by Neri di Bicci.

Opposite the church is **Antica Bottega**, a wine and cheese tasting bar, and beneath the arch a little further along is a traditional hole-in-the-wall called **Da' Vinattieri**, where you can try the Florentine speciality *trippa alla Fiorentina* – tripe with onions and tomatoes – if you have the stomach. This cobbled avenue is a quiet and charming place for a glass of *rosso* before leaving through the arch on to **Via del Corso** and turning right.

⓭ Take the first left, rejoining **Via dei Proconsolo**. Along this stretch you will pass the grand **Museo Nazionale di Antropologia ed Etnologia** (closed Wed) on your right, exhibiting anthropological artefacts from around the world. It is one of the six collections of the **Museo di Storia Naturale** which are dotted around the city. **Via Proconsolo** will take you back into **Piazza del Duomo**, where you can head into **Eduardo's** on your left for some hand-made *gelato*.

Museo Casa di Dante.

Da' Vinattieri.

The neighbouring towers of the Bargello and Badia Fiorentina.

29

Power and Patronage:
San Lorenzo to Santa Trinita

Florence, perhaps more than any other Italian city, was built on the patronage of the wealthy families to whom political power belonged from the 15thC onwards – in a city that was mostly a 'Republic' in name only. Often competing with each other, these families, whose fortunes were usually founded on commerce, poured their money into supporting artists, and the building of churches and *palazzi*. Pre-eminent among these were, of course, the Medici, the notorious dynasty who effectively ruled over Florence for nearly three centuries (excepting the odd bout of exile).

The Apotheosis of the Medici *(1680s) by Luca Giordano, in the Palazzo Medici.*

▶ **STARTS**
Palazzo Medici-Riccardi.

■ **ENDS**
Basilica di Santa Trinita.

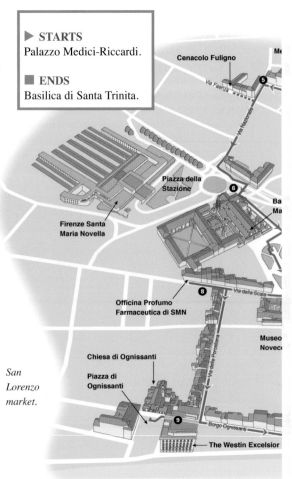

Cenacolo Fuligno

Via Faenza

Via Nazionale

5

Piazza della Stazione

6

Firenze Santa Maria Novella

Me

Ba
Ma

8

Via della Scala

Officina Profumo Farmaceutica di SMN

Museo
Novec

Interior of Basilica di Santa Maria Novella.

Chiesa di Ognissanti

Via delle Porcellana

Piazza di Ognissanti

San Lorenzo market.

9

Borgo Ognissanti

The Westin Excelsior

This walk begins at the Palazzo Medici, meandering through the diverse neighbourhoods of San Lorenzo and Santa Maria Novella via no less than three *palazzi* and four churches – all of them striking examples of how Renaissance oligarchs carved out their mark upon the fabric of the city, and illustrations of the symbiotic relationship between patronage, power and religion in Renaissance Florence. Along the way you'll wander through some of the best markets in Florence, sampling Tuscan delicacies and souvenirs, browsing centuries-old artisans and glitzy designer stores.

STARTS

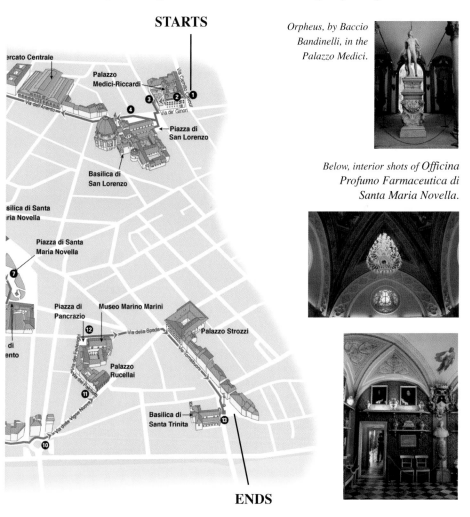

Orpheus, by Baccio Bandinelli, in the Palazzo Medici.

Below, interior shots of Officina Profumo Farmaceutica di Santa Maria Novella.

ENDS

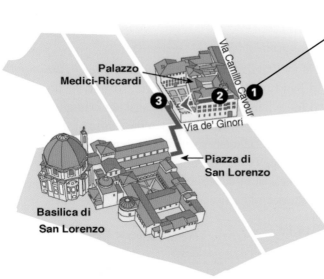

STARTS

Via Camillo Cavour

Palazzo
Medici-Riccardi

③ ② ①

Via de' Ginori

Piazza di
San Lorenzo

Basilica di
San Lorenzo

Below left, the garden courtyard of Palazzo Medici. Below centre, sketch of St Jerome's head on the back of the Madonna di Filippo Lippi, *in the Medici apartments. Below right, exterior of Palazzo Medici-Riccardi.*

❶ **Palazzo Medici-Riccardi (Via Camillo Cavour, 1**, closed Wed) was commissioned in 1444 by Cosimo Il Vecchio, the first of the Medici dynasty and *de facto* leader of Florence. Cosimo was a shrewd man, who understood he had to avoid ostentation in a city that called itself a 'Republic'. He therefore rejected Brunelleschi's grandiose design in favour of Michelozzo's sturdier alternative. Its features, such as the overhanging cornice and clearly delineated storeys (becoming more refined towards the upper storeys) set a precedent for *palazzos* in the 15thC. The design reflects the delicate balance of power Cosimo had to maintain: it was fairly small for such a wealthy family (though enlarged by Cosimo's more extravagant descendants), but the rusticated stone gave an intimidating, fortified impression – Cosimo's warning to potential rabble-rousers not to mess with the Medici.

Cosimo Il Vecchio as depicted in Benozzo Gozzoli's Magi Chapel.

Left, going clockwise: detail from Benozzo Gozzoli's Magi Chapel; the Galleria, with ceiling frescoes by Luca Giordano; the Medici Apartments. All upstairs in the Palazzo Medici-Riccardi.

2 Enter the elegant interior courtyard, crowded with heraldic Medici symbols. The staircase on your right leads to the **Magi Chapel** (buy tickets next door), painted by Benozzo Gozzoli in 1459. When Piero di Cosimo (known as Piero 'the Gouty') commissioned *The Journey of the Magi* he asked for the richest clothing to be depicted in the brightest possible colours, resulting in this beguiling fresco-cycle. Amidst its jewel-like splendour you nearly forget its religious subject. Gozzoli may have been inspired by the Council of Florence 20 years earlier, which drew to the city a host of Eastern delegates in their exotic apparel.

Wander through the rest of the sumptuous Medici apartments before returning to the courtyard, and from there enter the garden courtyard.

3 Leave through the garden courtyard, turning left on **Via de' Ginori**, which takes you into **Piazza di San Lorenzo**, with the **Basilica di San Lorenzo** on your right. Both the oldest and the largest basilica in Florence, it has a patchwork architectural history. The current church was mainly designed by Brunelleschi, though he died in 1446 before he could see it through, when the project was taken over by Manetti and Michelozzo (at the expense of the Medici). Michelangelo designed the beautiful **Laurentian Library** (enter to the left of the church door), which held the Medici's vast collection of antiquarian scripts.

The heraldic Medici Balls.

Interior of San Lorenzo.

Exterior of San Lorenzo.

The exterior of Mercato Centrale, and the market stalls inside.

4 Bear right, skirting the side of the church, and head straight down **Via dell'Ariento**, which hosts a street market selling leather goods. If you wish to sidestep pushy sellers go down the right-hand pavement, stopping at **Casa del Vino (no. 16R)**. This tiny historic wine bar attracts locals from about 9am onwards with its selection of Italian wines and cold-cuts. Further down you'll see the cast iron structure of **Mercato Centrale**, epicentre of Florence's food artisans and *the* place to go for authentic Tuscan cuisine. Wander the ground-floor stalls for fresh ingredients before heading upstairs to the cafe/restaurants pavilion (follow your nose for a dish of *pasta al tartufo* at **Il Tartufo**).

5 Go to the end of **Via dell'Ariento** and turn left down **Via Nazionale**. If you happen to be walking on a Monday or Wednesday take a detour right down **Via Faenza** to **Cenacolo Fuligno (no. 40)**, which holds Pietro Perugino's *The Last Supper* (also featured on **Last Supper Trail**, page 115). Otherwise, continue down **Via Nazionale** (**Sogni in Carta** *legatoria* at **no. 40** sells beautiful marbled notebooks). Emerge into the hectic **Piazza della Stazione** with the city's railway station on its right, which was hailed as an important example of 1930s Brutalist architecture.

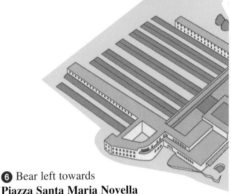

6 Bear left towards **Piazza Santa Maria Novella** and its eponymous basilica. This possesses one of the most iconic façades in Florence, designed by Alberti at the behest of the Rucellai family. Their family name (rooted in *oricello*, the red dye they imported) is emblazoned on the frieze, along with their emblem of a sail blowing in the wind (see picture, left). Giovanni Rucellai stipulated that the medieval lower half of the façade must be preserved, posing a dilemma to the 'uber'-humanist Alberti: the problem was neatly solved by the addition of scrolls, harmonizing the two halves of the façade to produce a Renaissance finish.

Inside you'll find Masaccio's *Trinity* (1428) thought to be one of the first truly Renaissance paintings because of the artist's use of the recently discovered technique of perspective, framed by the coffered ceiling of a triumphal arch. Head to Ghirlandaio's fresco-cycle in the main chapel (known as the **Tornabuoni Chapel**), painted 50 years later. His bravura use of perspective using classical architecture shows just how influential Masaccio truly was.

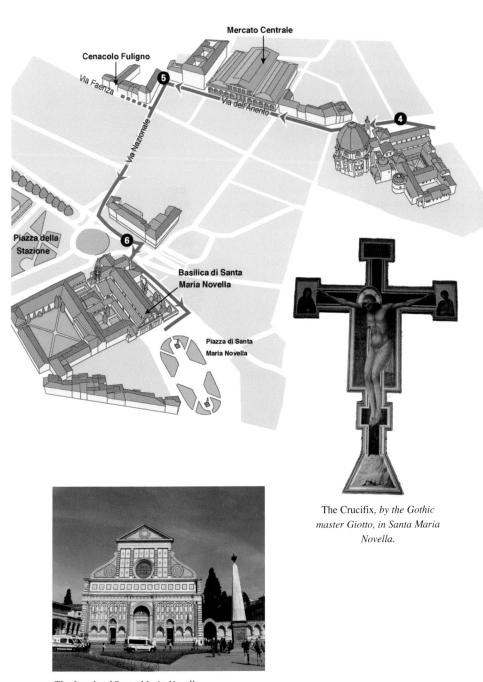

The Crucifix, *by the Gothic master Giotto, in Santa Maria Novella.*

The façade of Santa Maria Novella.

Interior of Officina Profuma Farmaceutica di Santa Maria Novella.

7 Cross the square towards **Museo Novecento**, a museum dedicated to the Italian art of the 20thC, and head right down **Via della Scala**, stopping at **Officina Profumo Farmaceutica di Santa Maria Novella** (**no. 16**). This was founded by Dominican friars around 1221, making it one of the oldest pharmacies in the world. In the 17thC word spread about the efficacy of the ointments and elixirs concocted by the friars, and the pharmacy was made public, earning widespread fame across Europe, Russia and even China. Today it is a verified museum, selling aromatic colognes, candles and teas, made from locally grown products and displayed in a lavish interior.

Fresco details in Officina Profumo Farmaceutica.

Priests robes exhibited in Officina Profumo Farmaceutica.

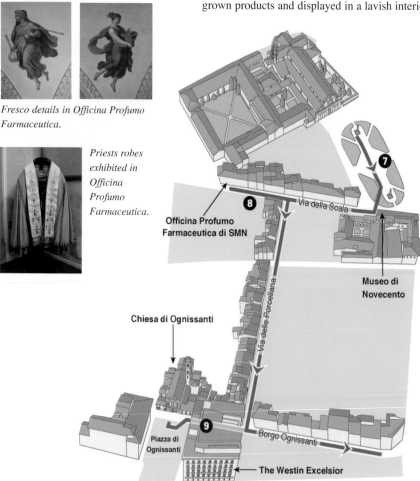

Interior of Officina Profumo.

Pietra dura (inlaid stone) altarpiece in Chiesa di Ognissanti.

Façade of Chiesa di Ognissanti.

Ceramic plate in Bottega D'Arte, on Borgo Ognissanti.

The Westin Excelsior Hotel.

8 Go left out of the Pharmacy, then take the first right down **Via delle Porcellana**. At the end of the street turn right down **Borgo Ognissanti**, which takes you to **Chiesa di Ognissanti**. Although brimming with wonderful art this church is often omitted by tourists. It's an absolute must for fans of Botticelli, the Renaissance master who lived in this neighbourhood most of his life, and worked here with Ghirlandaio in the 15thC. In the **Cappella Vespucci** (on the right wall of the nave) you'll find Ghirlandaio's *Madonna della Misericordia* (1472), in which the Madonna shelters members of the Vespucci family. The woman with the elaborate hairstyle on the right is Simonetta Vespucci, a renowned beauty with whom Botticelli fell madly in love, using her face for his famous depiction of Venus. When she died at the age of 23, Botticelli asked to be buried in this church in order to be near her. While the location of Simonetta's grave is lost, Botticelli's is commemorated by a circular marble slab in floor of the right transept.

Right, the Coats of Arms of wealthy families who patronized Chiesa di Ognissanti, dotted around its interior.

9 If you feel like an *aperol spritz* at this point, head to the top of the **Westin Excelsior** for a drink with panoramic views across Florence, before retracing your steps down **Borgo Ognissanti**. This delightful street hosts a number of artisans, including **Giovanni Baccani (no. 22)**, a stunning framer and print-seller; **Romano Antiques** next door; and **Bottega D'Arte (no. 3)**, a beautiful ceramicist originating from the 1300s.

A buchette del vino on Via dei Palchetti.

⑩ When you emerge into **Piazza Goldoni** take a left down **Via della Vigna Nuova**, the **Palazzo Rucellai** will appear after one block on your left. Designed by Alberti between 1446-51 for his long-term patron Giovanni Rucellai, it was one of the first to follow the trailblazing Palazzo Medici. Its construction required the demolition of an entire street of artisans (over a hundred *palazzos* would be built in the second half of the 15thC alone, dismantling whole neighbourhoods and radically changing the social landscape of the city). Alberti wanted to design a palace reflective of the new 'Athens on the Arno': one that was refined and delicate, unlike its fortress-like predecessor, hence his use of smooth stone and classical orders on each story.

Giovanni Baccani on Borgo Ognissanti.

⑪ Take a left down **Via dei Palchetti**, and you'll find **Il Latini** at **no. 6** – a highly recommendable trattoria, serving traditionally carnivorous dishes amid a bevy of noisy locals. To the bottom right of its entrance you'll see a *buchette del vino* (translating as 'small holes of wine', but also known as *tabernacoli del vino* because they look like little shrines). For centuries these were used by noble families to sell their wine to the public, being just big enough to pass through a litre bottle

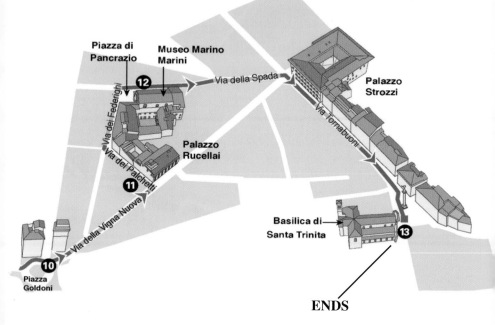

Piazza di Pancrazio

Museo Marino Marini

Via della Spada

Palazzo Strozzi

Via dei Federighi

⑫

Via Tornabuoni

Via dei Palchetti

Palazzo Rucellai

⑪

Via della Vigna Nuova

Basilica di Santa Trinita

⑬

⑩

Piazza Goldoni

ENDS

Left, the Palazzo Rucellai. Right, its stockier contemporary, Palazzo Strozzi.

covered in straw. The practice died out in the 20thC and most of them are now closed up. Take a right down **Via dei Federighi** and you enter **Piazza di Pancrazio**, where you'll find **Museo Marino Marini**, a former church now exhibiting works by the contemporary sculptor. Inside, a small area of sacred ground is preserved for the *Tempietto Santo Sepolcro* designed by Leon Battista Alberti to hold the sarcophagus of Giovanni Rucellai.

⑫ From the *piazza* take a right down **Via della Spada**. At the end, turn right down **Via Tornabuoni**, an elegant street lined with designer shops. **Procacci (no. 65)**, a hundred-year-old wine bar, serves delectable *tartufo panini*. The bottom of the street is dominated by the massive back of **Palazzo Strozzi**, built in 1489 for Filippo Strozzi. Filippo's son boastfully chronicled how his father tricked the Medici into allowing him to build such a grandiose palace by suggesting he'd had Lorenzo de' Medici's impeccable taste in mind when he drew up a design with Benedetto da Mariano. His sycophancy meant he avoided accusations of hubris from the ruling family, whilst getting the palace of his dreams.

Façade of Basilica di Santa Trinita.

Statue of Primavera (Spring) on Ponte Santa Trinita.

⑬ The **Basilica Santa Trinita** at the end of **Via Tornabuoni** is your final stop. It's home to the wonderful Sassetti Chapel – another fresco cycle by Ghirlandaio, depicting *The Life of St Francis*. Ghirlandaio's fresco cycles rarely feel as if they belong to a remote biblical past but rather to 15thC Italy, making him one of the most useful chroniclers of Renaissance Florence. For example, the scene of *St Francis Receiving the Order from Pope Honorius* is given a contemporary Roman setting, and attended by notable Florentines, including Lorenzo de Medici (on the right with the black hair, a flattering depiction of a man who was notoriously hideous) and of course Francesco Sassetti himself. Florentine patrons habitually inserted themselves into the artwork they commissioned: piety thinly veiled as an expression of power to the many citizens who would come to pray before them – an apt endpoint to a trail exploring power and patronage.

Walking with Ghosts: Santa Croce

Madonna and Child Enthroned *by Lorenzo di Niccolò (1409) in the Basilica di Santa Croce.*

Ghosts of Florence past stalk the streets and monuments of Santa Croce. Be they in the Basilica di Santa Croce, resting place to a host of illustrious Florentines (earning it the local nickname of 'The Pantheon'), or Casa Buonarroti, dedicated to the legacy of Michelangelo, the city's most renowned sculptor – or simply the place names themselves, from Piazza Lorenzo Ghiberti to Via Andrea del Verocchio.

In fact, you'll find much more than echoes of historic Florentines in this neighbourhood. Its both popular with visitors and local in feel, steeped in history as well as being a hotspot for Florentine nightlife. In other words, there's something for everyone. This is one of the most varied walks, taking in two churches, two museums, multiple restaurants, a daily food market, and finishing off with the Great Synagogue of Florence: one of the city's most distinctive buildings, it is also one that often escapes the tourist radar.

Far left, the Sinagoga. Left, Basilica di Santa Croce.

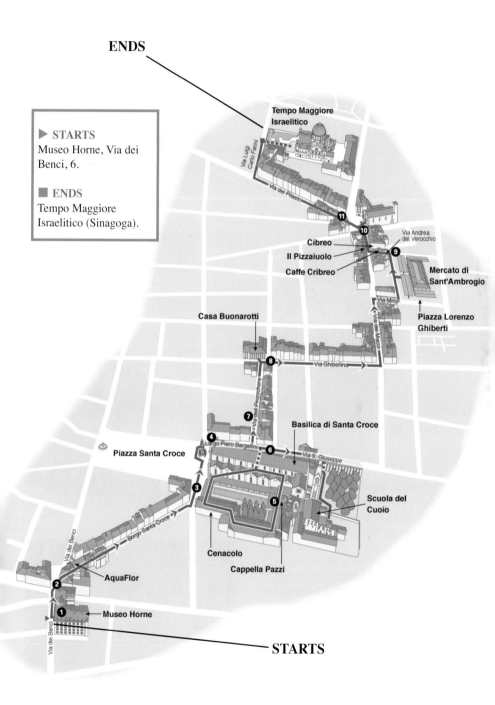

ENDS

▶ STARTS
Museo Horne, Via dei
Benci, 6.

■ ENDS
Tempo Maggiore
Israelitico (Sinagoga).

Tempo Maggiore
Israelitico

Via Luigi
Carlo Farini

Via dei Pilastri

Cibreo
Il Pizzaiuolo
Caffe Cribreo

Via Andrea
del Verocchio

Mercato di
Sant'Ambrogio

Via Mino

Piazza Lorenzo
Ghiberti

Casa Buonarotti

Via dei Macci

Via Ghibellina

Basilica di Santa Croce

Via dell'Pinzochere

Piazza Santa Croce

Largo Piero Bargellini

Via S. Giuseppe

Scuola del
Cuoio

Via dei Benci

Borgo Santa Croce

Cenacolo

Cappella Pazzi

AquaFlor

Museo Horne

STARTS

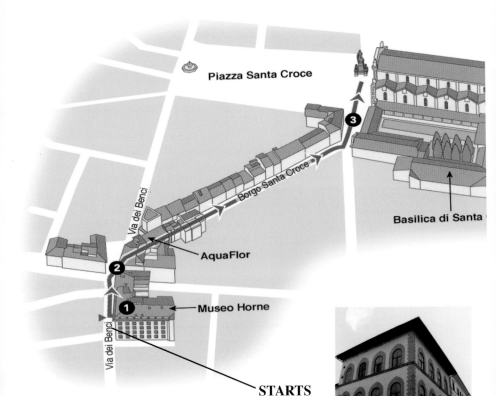

Museo Horne.

❶ The **Museo Horne** at **Via dei Benci, 6** is named after the Englishman Herbert Percy Horne. A Renaissance Man in his own time (living between 1864-1916) he was a poet, architect, typographer, art historian and antiquarian. He moved to Florence after first visiting Italy in 1889, spending years restoring this 15thC *palazzo* to its original Renaissance splendour, before moving in and filling it with his magpie collection of art and furniture. His collection spans the Gothic and Renaissance periods, and includes modest pieces by Botticelli and Giambologna. Enjoy the grand apartments in splendid isolation, as the museum is usually empty.

Piano Nobile of Museo Horne.

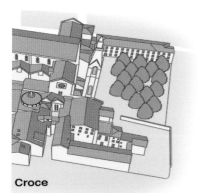

Croce

A 'desco da parto' - birth tray - in Museo Horne, painted between 1450-1475 by Domenico di Zanobi: the traditional Italian gift to celebrate a healthy birth.

The Neo-Gothic façade of Basilica di Santa Croce.

❷ Outside **Museo Horne**, turn right down **Via dei Benci**, and right again down **Borgo Santa Croce**. Soon the mellifluous scent from **AquaFlor** at **no. 6** will reach your nostrils. Set in an elegant 16thC *palazzo*, the *profumeria* exudes all the mystery and ambience you'd expect from one that uses more than 1,500 ingredients to create its perfumes, using techniques dating back to the 15thC, when Florentine scientists were obsessed with extracting scent from plants.

❸ At the end of **Via dei Benci** you'll arrive in **Piazza Santa Croce**, with the 19thC neo-Gothic façade of the **Basilica di Santa Croce** on your right. The *piazza's* size has long leant it to public events, beginning with pageants celebrating noble marriages during the Medici era. Today, a field of sand with surrounding stands is prepared every June for Calcio Fiorentino, the notoriously bloody football tournament played between the four historic neighbourhoods of Florence (Santo Spirito were the reigning champions as the guide went to press). During the day the historic *piazza* is flocked with tourists visiting the basilica, and by night it becomes a nexus for nightlife, as the church's steps fill will revellers overflowing from the *piazza's* bars. We'd recommend the rustic wine bar **Dondino** at **no. 6**, and **Ristorante Boccadama** at **no. 25**, ideal for romantic candlelit dinners.

AquaFlor.

43

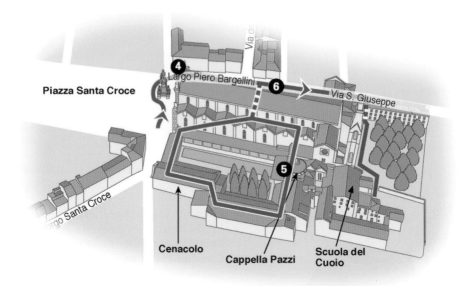

4 Skirt around the imperious statue of Dante – sculpted by Enrico Pazzi in 1865 to commemorate the 600th anniversary of the poet's birth – and go along **Largo Piero Bargellini**. In the *loggia* at the side of the church you'll find its ticket office and entrance. This basilica was rebuilt for the Franciscans in 1294 to compete with their Dominican rivals in **Santa Maria Novella**. Inside its gloomy interior memorials clog the walls, marking the burial places of luminaries such as Galileo Galilei, Machiavelli and Michelangelo (whose Baroque tomb is particularly lurid

The Santa Croce Altarpiece, painted by Ugolino di Nerio between 1325-8.

The nave of Santa Croce.

and overbearing). It boasts a wealth of art, spread across its 16 frescoed chapels (Giotto's **Bardi Chapel** being the most famous) and the **Museo dell'Opera di Santa Croce**, located next door.

5 Wandering the caverns of Santa Croce could easily take up a morning, but the **Pazzi Chapel**, located in the first cloister of its southern flank, is often considered to be its greatest treasure. It was designed by Brunelleschi as a private oratory for the Pazzi family, who are remembered for conspiring against the Medici family in 1478. While Giuliano de Medici was killed his brother Lorenzo escaped, and when the dust settled the Pazzis were exiled, making the Medici more powerful than ever. Despite the Pazzis turbulent history,

Tomb of Michelangelo (d. 1564), designed by Vasari in 1570; three sculptures personifying Painting, Sculpture and Architecture.

The tomb of Galileo Galilei (d. 1642). Florence had to wait a century before erecting it, so to not incur the wrath of Pope Urban VIII, who pronounced his heliocentric theory heretical.

The Memorial Monument to Carlo Marsuppini (d. 1453), an important Florentine official, and teacher to Piero and Lorenzo de Medici.

Above, the exterior and interior of the Pazzi Chapel, designed by Brunelleschi.

their chapel is renowned as one of the purest expressions of Renaissance harmony and balance. With its perfect train of *pietra serena* arches, held up by elegant Corinthian pilasters and mounted by a perfect dome, it's also Brunelleschi's most quintessential monument, while others such as San Lorenzo have been mongrelized by other hands.

Head to the refectory and you'll find Taddeo Gaddi's weird yet wonderful *Crucifixion* and *Last Supper* (discussed in detail on **Last Supper Trail**, page 112).

❻ Leave the church and head back down **Largo Piero Bargellini**, which merges on to **Via S. Giuseppe.** You'll find the entrance to the **Scuola del Cuoio** at **no. 5**, attached to the rear of the basilica. This Leather School was founded in 1950 by a group of Franciscan friars, with the objective of giving an occupation to young people orphaned by the Second World War. Now you can wander through the workshop to watch the apprentices at work, and browse top-quality leather souvenirs made on site.

Right, a leather worker in the Scuola del Cuoio, and the school's courtyard.

Left, The Allegory of Inclination *(1616) by Artemisia Gentileschi, who is considered to have been one of the most accomplished followers of Caravaggio. The allegory was commissioned by Michelangelo the Younger to personify his grand-uncle's natural talent. By making it a self-portrait, Artemisia obliquely alludes to her own natural talent as well – a bold move for a female painter during this period.*

The Galleria of Casa Buonarotti.

The Battle of the Centaurs *(1492), a relief sculpture by Michelangelo. He regarded it as the best of his early works.*

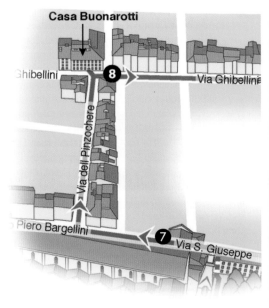

7 Outside the entrance to the **Leather School**, take a left back down **Via S. Giuseppe**, then third right down **Via dell Pinzochere**. You'll emerge on to **Via Ghibellini**, with the **Casa Buonarroti** (historic home of Michelangelo's family) straight ahead at **no. 70**. Despite being the city's most internationally renowned artist, Michelangelo was also its most atypical: his proto-Baroque style flew in the face of Florentine balance and restraint, which is perhaps why he spent most of his life in Rome carrying out the hubristic projects of tyrannical popes. This museum is a rare Baroque enclave in the city, dripping in gilded stucco carvings and dramatic oil paintings. It exhibits works by the master himself – including the lovely relief *Madonna della Scala*, his homage to Donatello – as well as the historic collection of the Buonarroti family.

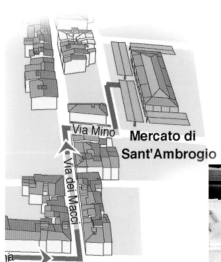

Sant'Ambrogio Market.

Fresh produce, spices and
market stalls in Mercato
Sant'Ambrogio.

❽ Outside the museum take a left down **Via Ghibellina**, then
the third left down **Via dei Macci** (dropping in to **Leonardo's**
at **no. 65** for some homemade *biscotti*). After two blocks, turn
right down **Via Mino**, which takes you into **Piazza Lorenzo
Ghiberti**. This is home to **Sant'Ambrogio Market** (open daily
between 7am-2pm), essentially a smaller version of **Mercato
Centrale**, with a more local feel. Inside (beyond the
unappealing clothes stores) you'll find countless stalls selling
fresh poultry, cheese, meat and vegetables, as well as pop-up
trattorias if you wish to stop for lunch, or stand with the locals
for a drink.

⑨ Head down **Via Andrea del Verocchio** at the corner of the *piazza* (with **Lisa Corti**, the beautiful textile store, at **no. 33**). Here you enter **Cibréo** territory, with the **Caffe Cibréo** on your left at **no. 5**, a cosy walnut interior hung with vintage prints, and the flagship restaurant opposite at **no. 8**. Take a right down **Via dei Macci** (walking past the highly recommendable **Il Pizzaiuolo** at **no. 113**) and the **Trattoria Cibréo** (its cheaper and more rustic sister establishment) will be on the right side at **no. 122**. It's well worth visiting one of these during your stay: Cibréo is highly celebrated in Florence, offering a traditional menu that changes daily depending on what the chefs buy in Sant'Ambrogio market that morning.

⑩ Via dei Macci will take you into **Piazza Sant'Ambrogio**, with the **Chiesa di Sant'Ambrogio** on your right. Reportedly built where Saint Ambrose stayed in 393 AD, the church was first recorded in 998 AD. Its status was insignificant and parochial until 1230, when a priest alleged he'd found an uncleaned chalice containing blood instead of wine. The miracle turned the church into a place of pilgrimage, accounting for the number of lovely art works gracing its modest interior, including pieces by Masaccio, Filippo Lippi and Botticelli.

Chiesa di Sant'Ambrogio.

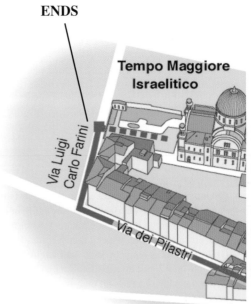

Caffe Cibréo.

Lisa Corti.

Lady Jane B.

11 Cross the *piazza* and head down **Via dei Pilastri** (vintage clothing enthusiasts should pop into **Lady Jane B** at **no. 32**). Take a right down **Via Luigi Carlo Farini**, and you'll find **Ruth's** on the right at **no. 2** – a homely Jewish restaurant serving up comforting mezze platters of falafels, humus and grilled vegetables. Further along at **no. 6** you'll find the **Tempo Maggiore Israelitico**, perched like a miniature Taj Mahal in its exotic gardens. The synagogue was built in the 19thC, and designed to evoke oriental splendour: every inch of its spellbinding interior is hand-painted with hypnotic red and blue designs, leading the eye up to a magnificent dome, sheathed in shiny copper. Its museum tells the story of the synagogue, which was used as a garage by Nazi occupiers, and desecrated upon their retreat (the doors of the Holy Arc still bear the scars from Nazi bayonets), as well as the history of the Jewish community in Florence.

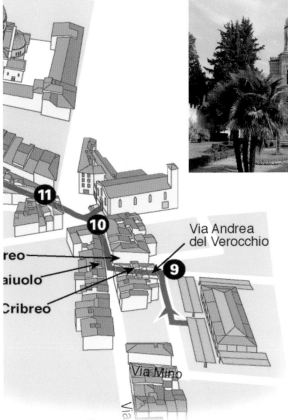

The exterior of the Sinagoga.

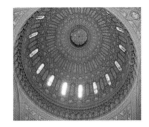

The Sinagoga's copper-sheathed dome.

Sacred Spaces: San Marco

The neighbourhood of San Marco is imbued with a peculiar calm – a sense of being on the outskirts, whilst being a mere stone's throw from Florence's busy cathedral *piazza*. It's a useful transport hub (most bus lines leave from here), as well as the principal university district, which may account for the scholarly hush that pervades.

    The sublime artwork on this route, found nestled within the convents of San Marco, Sant'Apollonia and Chiostro dello Scalzo, as well as the Basilica SS Annunziata with its 'miraculous' painting of the Annunciation, could convert even the most stalwart atheist – but religious art is by no means the only thing on the menu. The walk takes you through the Giardino dei Semplici, a tropical garden dating back to the 16thC; Piazza SS Annunziata, one of the first purpose-built Renaissance spaces in the city, with its Foundling Hospital designed by Brunelleschi; and last, but manifestly not least, the Galleria dell'Accademia, home to Michelangelo's iconic *David*. The circuit is short, but its attractions could easily take all day. We recommend starting in the morning, while the convents are still open, before spending a leisurely afternoon in the Accademia – what could be better? If possible, do the walk on a Monday or Thursday, when the Chiostro dello Scalzo is open.

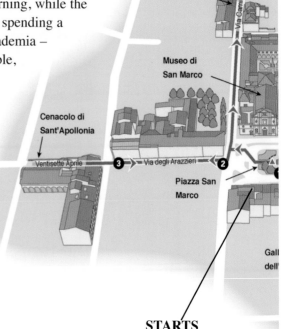

The Basilica di San Marco.

STARTS

Michelangelo's David.

Left and below, the Giardino dei Semplici.

▶ **STARTS**
Piazza San Marco.

■ **ENDS**
Galleria dell'Accademia.

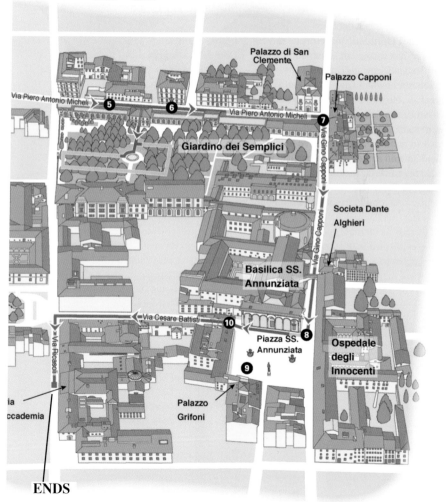

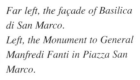

Far left, the façade of Basilica di San Marco.
Left, the Monument to General Manfredi Fanti in Piazza San Marco.

Left, detail from Fra Angelico's Annunciation.

❶ Begin in **Piazza San Marco**, with the *Monument To General Manfredo Fanti*, a hero of Italian Unification, at its centre. The *piazza* is dominated by the 18thC neo-classical façade of the **Basilica San Marco**. The basilica itself dates back to the 12thC when it was founded as a Vallombrosian monastery, until Cosimo Il Vecchio de Medici handed it over to the Dominicans in 1437. In the same period the Medici appointed their favourite architect, Michelozzo, to rebuild the church. Today it's free to enter, but the real attraction (for which there is an entrance fee) is **Museo di San Marco** located in its convent (open Mon-Fri between 8.15am-1.50pm, and Sat-Sun between 8.15am-4.50pm), which is largely devoted to the ethereal frescoes of the 15thC monk Fra Angelico. Known in his lifetime as Beato Angelico (Blessed Angelic One) he was so pious that he allegedly wept whilst painting the Crucifixion. Inside you can find cells of the monastery's more illustrious alumni, starting with Cosimo Il Vecchio (the first Medici leader), who was given a complimentary cell to pray in as a thank you for his patronage (arguably a wily PR move on Cosimo's part). Later, San Marco became the stronghold for extremist monk Savonarola, who led the theocracy that ruled Florence between 1494 and 1498. Through his inflammatory sermons he incited Florentines to burn their worldly goods on his Bonfires of Vanity. He was eventually burned himself in Piazza della Signoria – in a city of natural aesthetes, his asceticism could only be tolerated for so long.

Frescoes by Fra Angelico in the Museo di San Marco. Far left, The Coronation of the Virgin. *Left,* Noli me Tangere *(when the resurrected Jesus appears before Mary Magdalene).*

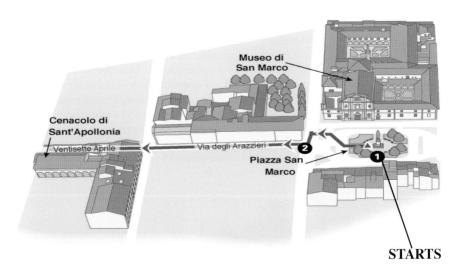

STARTS

The Last Supper
by Andrea del Castagno.

*Plinth of the Monument to General
Manfredo Fanti.*

❷ Facing the church, bear left down **Via degli Arrazieri**. When this merges on to **Via Ventisette Aprile** you'll find **Cenacolo Sant'Apollonia** on your left at **no. 1** (open daily between 8.15-13.50). This little-known gem – a Benedictine nunnery founded in 1339 – holds a seminal *Last Supper* by the 15thC master Andrea del Castagno (this also features on the **Last Supper Trail**, page 114). Painted between 1445 and 1450, for centuries this was enjoyed by the nuns alone, until 1866 when the convent was suppressed and the fresco made public (accounting for its current mint condition). As is typical of early representations, Castagno shows the apostles lined up on one side of the table, whilst Judas is singled out on the other,

with his characteristic dark hair, sallow complexion and a hook nose. In other ways he's made a Renaissance leap forward by setting the figures in an expertly painted architectural hollow, using perspective to draw the viewer in. The psychedelic panel behind Jesus is in fact a lightening bolt erupting from the sky to hail Judas as a traitor.

The Virgin with Child and Saints
by Neri di Bicci, in Sant'Apollonia.

SACRED SPACES: SAN MARCO

❸ Retrace your steps to **Piazza San Marco** and head north up **Via Camillo Cavour**. The modest façade of **Chiostro dello Scalzo** will appear on your left at **no. 69** (open Mondays, Thursdays and the 1st, 3rd and 5th Saturday of the month, 8.15am-1.50pm). Formerly used by the Brothers of the Company of John the Baptist, it was nicknamed 'Dello Scalzo' – meaning 'Cloister of the Barefoot' – because the monks did processions barefoot in imitation of John's vow of poverty. Its small courtyard is decorated by one of the most unique fresco cycles from the 16thC by Andrea del Sarto, famed in his lifetime as an artist *senza error* ('without error'). His popularity diminished in later times, perhaps because of what modern audiences consider his slightly anodyne perfection – but there is nothing anodyne about these frescoes, depicting the life of John the Baptist in a startling monochrome grisaille style. The frescoes had a huge formative influence on the development of Mannerism.

The Baptism of the People *by Andrea del Sarto, painted in 1517 for the Chiostro Dello Scalzo.*

Above, the Porta S Gallo (1285) in Piazza della Liberta; right, the Triumphal Arch of Lorraine opposite it.

❹ Continue down **Via Camillo Cavour**. At this point your route takes a right down **Via Piero Antonio Micheli**, although it is worth mentioning that if you continued down **Via Camillo Cavour** you'd eventually arrive in **Piazza della Liberta**: unpleasantly congested with traffic but nonetheless an interesting place in Florentine history. The **Triumphal Arch of Lorraine** at its centre was built in 1737 to welcome the Hapsburg-Lorraines, ushered in as rulers when the heir-less Gian Gastone de Medici died. It's the same arch through which they were exiled in 1859. The *piazza* itself (which marks the most northerly point of the city's historic centre) was built in 1875 as one of six new Viale di Ciconvallaziones – boulevards in the Parisian style – built on the outline of the old city walls, in an attempt to modernize the city. Ever true to their Renaissance roots, Florentines have relegated it both physically and symbolically to the

Far left, centre and below, in the Giardino dei Semplici.

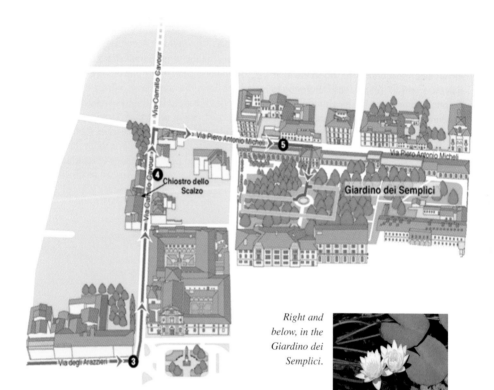

Right and below, in the Giardino dei Semplici.

outskirts, and use it as a glorified roundabout. If you take this detour, retrace your steps down **Via Camillo Cavour** and take a left down **Via Piero Antonio Micheli.**

5 Continue down **Via Piero Antonio Micheli** and you'll reach **Giardino dei Semplici**, a tropical garden incongruously plonked in the middle of residential San Marco (the entrance is found at **no. 3 Via Piero Antonio Micheli**). Cosimo I seized the land from Dominican nuns in 1545 in order to cultivate and research exotic plants. Essential oils were extracted to make perfumes, medicines and poisons (poison being the preferred method of assassination by Medici princes). Today its multifarious attractions include a greenhouse storing carnivorous plants (distinguished by the aroma of rotting flesh), a classic Italianate garden and a Japanese garden.

6 Leave the gardens and turn right, continuing down **Via Pier Antonio Micheli**. At the corner on the left you'll see **Palazzo di San Clemente** (**no. 2**), a *casini* (city villa) designed in the 17thC by Gherardo Silvani, the architect of Chiesa dei San Gaetano and Palazzo Corsini. Silvani was influenced by Tuscan Mannerism (a more experimental offshoot of the Renaissance) whilst rejecting the more elaborate style of Baroque, which was flourishing in Rome during this period. Due to the naturally restrained Florentine character, this was the closest they came to a native Baroque style. It now houses the **Florence University Architecture Department.**

7 Turn right down **Via Gino Capponi**, past the **Palazzo Gino Capponi** on your left (**no. 26**) – sadly closed to the public, its grandiose gardens just glimpsable through its driveway. This rundown residential street also hosts a number of university departments. At **no. 7** you'll see the crumbling courtyard of the Department of Geography, Archeology, Art History, and at **no. 4** on your left the **Societa Dante Alighieri**, which teaches Italian and promotes the language throughout the world – one of the oldest societies of its kind. Enter its tiny cloister – so-called 'Chiostro di S. Piero' – to see its fresco cycle of the *Life of St Peter.*

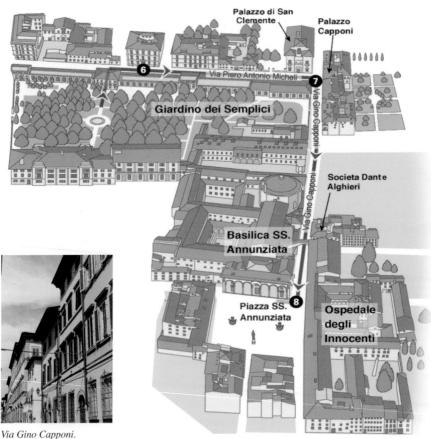

Via Gino Capponi.

8 **Via Gino Capponi** will take you into **Piazza della Santissima Annunziata**, a tranquil *piazza* that is rich in history. Its **Basilica Santissima Annunziata** became famous when a miracle allegedly occurred here in 1252: the story goes that a resident monk abandoned his painting of the Annunciation, frustrated in capturing the subject's true beauty, only to wake up in the morning and find it finished by the hand of an angel. As pilgrims flocked from all over the world, the church grew in size and grandeur, resulting in a complete redesign by Michelozzo in 1444, a later 17thC Baroque makeover, and the acquisition of artworks by

The Basilica Santissima Annunziata.

Andrea del Sarto and Pontormo.

In the 15thC, the church's reputation galvanised plans to spruce up its *piazza*, making this the first purpose-built Renaissance square. Work kicked off in 1419 with Brunelleschi's **Ospedale degli Innocenti**. Its elegant *loggia* with nine semi-circular arches reflects his ideals of proportion and harmony, and the move towards Classicised architecture. The blue and white terracotta roundels in its spandrels

Loggia of the Ospedale Innocenti.

Above, the Ospedale degli Innocenti. Left, the grated window through which foundlings were deposited.

(by Andrea della Robbia) depict babies in swaddling clothes, reflecting the function of the hospital: to take in the city's abandoned children. Head to the north end of the *loggia* and you'll find two frescoed babies holding a scroll that reads: 'Our fathers and mothers have abandoned us, but the lord has taken us' (Psalm 27:10). Below is a grated window, the gaps in its bars just big enough to pass a baby through, in order to entrust it to the care of the Innocenti (the practice continued until 1875). Inside, a touching museum tells the orphanage's story alongside works of art by Botticelli and Ghirlandaio.

One of the terracotta roundels by Andrea della Robbia, on the façade of the hospital.

⑨ The **Palazzo Grifoni** (opposite the Basilica) was built by the Tuscan Mannerist Bartolomeo Ammanati, and completed by Buontalenti. A number of myths have accrued about its always-open top-right window, the most enduring being that of wife who waited by the window for her husband to return from a 16thC war until the day she died. Afterwards, her family were haunted by a frenzy of noise and disruption every time they tried to close it. At the centre of the *piazza* is the equestrian statue of *Ferdinando I de' Medici* by Giambologna, made from the melted-down bronze of canons – the swarm of bees at its base is meant to symbolize the ruler's leadership skills and his industrious followers.

Above, the equestrian statue of Ferdinando I de' Medici. Far right, the Palazzo Grifoni. Right, one of the two demonic fountains in Piazza SS Annunziata, cast by the Mannerist sculptor Pietro Tacca in the 17thC.

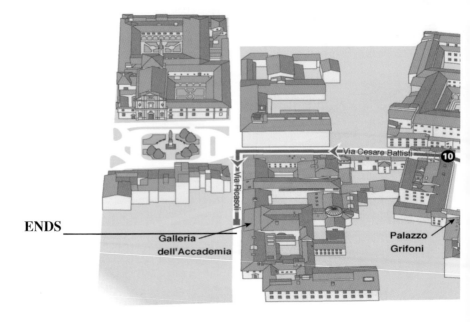

ENDS

Galleria
dell'Accademia

Palazzo
Grifoni

⑩ Via Cesare Battisti, at the corner of the Basilica, will take you back to **Piazza San Marco**, at which point you take an immediate left down **Via Ricasoli**. The **Galleria dell'Accademia** will appear very soon on your left at **no. 58-60**. The reason for the hefty queue is of course Michelangelo's *David*. It's no accident this has become one of the most iconic artworks in the city: David, who defeated the mighty Goliath, has always been seen as a potent symbol of Florence – small but strong, cerebral as well as beautiful. While the sculpture might appear a model of human perfection, his head is in fact disproportionately large, symbolising a brain that equals brawn. The sculpture's perfection was considered even more extraordinary because Michelangelo used a 'ruined' piece of marble, already hacked away at by his inferior contemporary, Giambologna.

While this is the Accademia's most famous attraction by far, and rightly given pride of place, the galleries hold a whole roster of masterpieces, including Michelangelo's unfinished *Slaves* and two Madonnas by Botticelli. An afternoon is, in fact, not enough to do it justice.

Above, Michelangelo's David *in the Galleria dell'Accademia. Below, anatomical drawing outside the Florence Academy of Fine Arts, next door to the Accademia.*

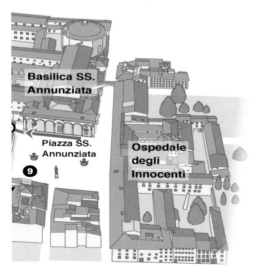

Living it up with the Locals: Oltrarno

▶ **STARTS**
Southern end of
Ponte Vecchio.

■ **ENDS**
Ponte Vecchio.

The Oltrarno (literally meaning 'beyond the Arno') could easily become your favourite part of Florence. It may not boast the Uffizi or Accademia (which is not to say it's bereft of beautiful art – barely a square metre of Florence is, after all) but wandering its streets brings you closer to the heart of Florentine life than a human traffic-jam by the Duomo ever could. Despite the very real threat of gentrification (not to mention the disastrous flood of 1966) a great number of artisans in this district are alive and kicking, originally enticed here in the 15thC when the Medici family – the most sought-after customers in the city – moved into the Palazzo Pitti. As you walk, keep your eyes peeled and don't be afraid to ring the doorbells of seemingly closed workshops: these centuries-old artisan operations favour word-of-mouth over advertising.

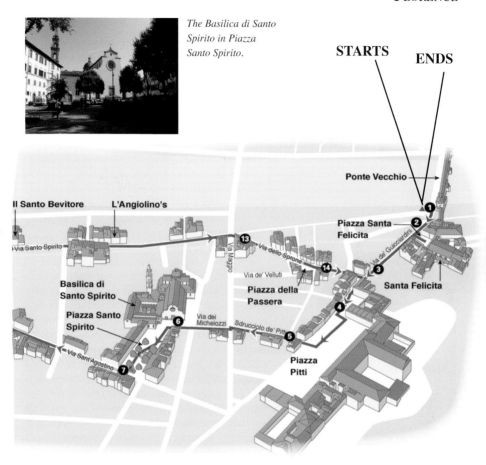

The Basilica di Santo Spirito in Piazza Santo Spirito.

Besides workshops this circuit will introduce you to the neighbourhoods of Santo Spirito and San Frediano. It's also a gastronomic route, passing several of the best restaurants in the city. You'll get a healthy dose of churches (all free to enter) as well as the Cappella Brancacci, home to Masaccio's world famous masterpiece. The district has also gained a reputation as a Bohemian enclave, and has spawned a host of trendy bars (explored more fully in **La Dolce Vita** on page 80).

The traditional artisans as well as the churches on this walk tend to close for *siesta*, between 12.30-3.30pm, so to avoid disappointment try to do this walk in the morning or later in the afternoon (the golden hours of 3.30-5.30pm, when both churches and artisans are open). Also avoid Sundays and Mondays, when the majority of stores will be closed.

The Manelli Tower on the southern end of the Ponte Vecchio.

❶ Begin at the southern end of the **Ponte Vecchio**. This is the oldest bridge in Florence, dating back to 1345 when it replaced a Roman predecessor destroyed in a flood. Historically, it has accommodated all manner of vendors, but Duke Ferdinando I de Medici was so offended by the smell produced (especially by the butchers) that in 1593 he decreed only goldsmiths could trade on the bridge, a tradition that's held to this day. The **Vasari corridor**, which runs across the top of the bridge, was built in 1565 so that Duke Cosimo I de' Medici could avoid walking with hoi polloi on the street when travelling from the Palazzo Vecchio to his home at the Palazzo Pitti.

The interior of Basilica di Santa Felicita.

The Deposition *by Jacopo Pontormo.*

❷ Head down **Via de' Guicciardini**, and left into **Piazza Santa Felicita**, with its eponymous basilica straight ahead. Here, the **Vasari Corridor** runs through the church's façade, above the main portal. This enabled the Grand Dukes of the Medici family to attend mass, listening through a window covered by a grate, unseen by the crowds at ground level. The basilica itself is the oldest in the city after San Lorenzo, originally built in the 2ndC by Syrian Greek merchants, who are thought to have brought Christianity to the region. The church's undisputed masterpiece, which has resided here for the past 500 years, is Jacopo Pontormo's *Deposition*. Painting in the Mannerist style of the 16thC, Pontormo radically broke from the balanced compositions and measured realism of the Renaissance, instead distorting reality for emotional effect. The foreground is

Above, detail from The Deposition. *Right, Pontormo's* Annunciation.

uncomfortably congested with bodies, their complexions rendered sallow by Pontormo's acerbic colour palette, while two horrified figures crumple beneath the exaggerated weight of the dead Christ as he is lowered from the cross. As if providing a balm for this harrowing scene, Pontormo painted a strikingly beautiful *Annunciation* on the side of the chapel.

❸ Continue down **Via de' Guicciardini** and you come into **Piazza Pitti**, with the monumental **Palazzo Pitti** on your left, built originally for the Florentine banker Luca Pitti. Its size and grandeur overshadows all the *palazzi* in Florence, which is why the Medici – Florence's most powerful family for three centuries – felt compelled to buy it for themselves in 1549. It is now home to the **Palatine Gallery**, a stunning collection of over 500 paintings, as well as lesser known collections of porcelain, silver and fashion.

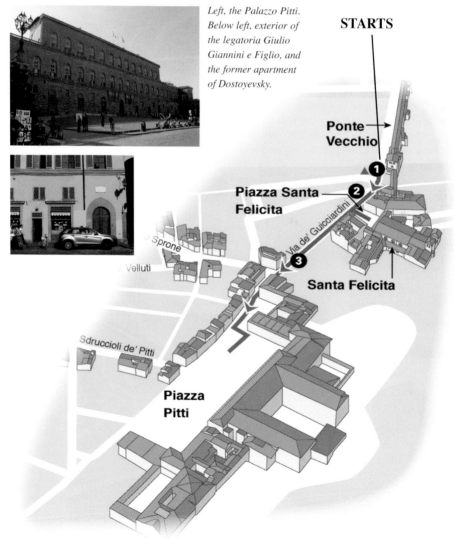

Left, the Palazzo Pitti. Below left, exterior of the legatoria Giulio Giannini e Figlio, and the former apartment of Dostoyevsky.

STARTS

Ponte Vecchio

Piazza Santa Felicita

Via de' Guicciardini

Sprone

Velluti

Santa Felicita

Sdruccioli de' Pitti

Piazza Pitti

The interior of Giulio Giannini e Figlio.

④ Our artisanal tour of the Oltrarno also begins in **Piazza Pitti**. To the right as you enter is **Giulio Giannini e Figlio (no. 37)**, established here in 1856 as a bookbinder and stationer. At that time bookbinding and marbling paper were being established as Florentine specialities, to cater for Englishmen on their Grand Tour. The great Russian author Fyodor Dostoyevsky stayed next door between 1861 and 1869 to finish his novel *The Idiot*. **Pitti Mosaici** at **no. 23r** specializes in the equally archetypical Florentine art of *pietre dure*: the ancient technique of inlaying different coloured stones to create pictures.

A handpainted map in La Casa della Stampa.

Statue of Cosimo Ridolfi.

Marbled paper in La Casa della Stampa.

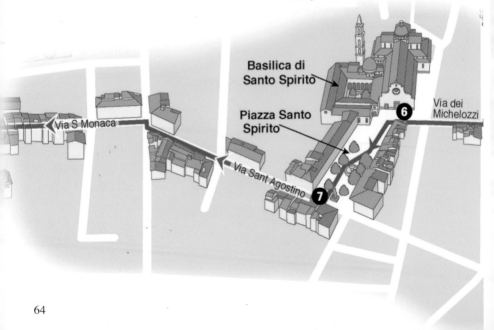

View of Piazza Santo Spirito.

5 Take a right down **Srduccioli de' Pitti**, home to a number of charming shops including **La Casa della Stampa** at **no. 11**, a delightful antique print seller. Continue in this direction, merging on to **Via dei Michelozzi**, where you'll find **Gustapizza** (one of the best – and cheapest – pizzerias in the city. If you feel like a more casual dining experience, get your order in amid vociferous locals and eat in the *piazza*). Now enter **Piazza Santo Spirito**, undoubtedly the epicentre of activity in Oltrarno. It attracts an eclectic crowd, including salt-of-the-earth locals, Bohemian expats and a number of homeless men who congregate around the fountain. It's laced with a slew of café-cum-bars, and there's usually a market selling cheap clothes and fresh ingredients.

6 Enter the **Basilica di S. Maria del Santo Spirito** and you'll find an interior that perfectly encapsulates the precepts of Renaissance architecture – as you'd expect from its architect, Brunelleschi, the man responsible for the city's formidable dome, who was obsessed by the harmony of mathematics.

The fountain in Piazza Santo Spirito.

The façade of Basilica di Santo Spirito.

7 Come out of the church and cross the square, bearing right. **Osteria di Santo Spirito**, on the corner of the *piazza* and **Via S. Agostino**, makes the best *gnocchi al tartufo* in the city, served in a spitting hot dish. Head down **Via S Agostino** (**Legatoria S. Agostino, no. 15**, is one of the cheaper suppliers of marbled stationary). At the crossroads, continue in the same direction down **Via S. Monaca** (worthy pit stops include **Panificio** at **no. 3**, drawing customers in with the saccharine scent of freshly baked tarts, and an atmospheric wine bar called **Vivanda** at **no.7**).

Via de

Sdruccioli de' Pitti

Piazza de' Pitti

Masolino's Temptation of Adam and Eve *on the far left, versus Masaccio's* Expulsion of Adam and Eve *on the left. Right, detail from the Corsini Chapel.*

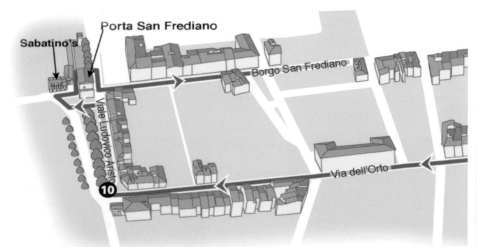

Far left to right: the interior of Chiesa Santa Maria del Carmine; the exterior; detail from the Brancacci Chapel.

❽ Via S. Monaca takes you into **Piazza del Carmine**, with the plain façade of **Chiesa Santa Maria del Carmine** on your left. Founded in 1268, it was gutted by a fire in 1771, resulting in a late Baroque makeover. In a city that was stubbornly inclined towards the balance and order of the Renaissance, the **Corsini Chapel** in the left transept is a rare jewel of Florentine Baroque art. However, the real gem of this complex is the **Cappella Brancacci**, entered to the right of the main portal, containing a fresco cycle of *The Life of St Peter* by Masolino and Masaccio. Despite his age, the Gothic master Masolino (who painted the right side of the

Porta San Frediano.

chapel) adapted his style to match the younger, more innovative Masaccio, who was in many ways the father of the Renaissance – one of the first to carve out space in paint through the use of perspective. You can gauge the difference by contrasting their two depictions of Adam and Eve: Masolino's seems elegant yet vapid when compared to Masaccio's stalwart figures on the opposite wall, contorted in anguish as they are expelled from the Garden of Eden. Don't forget to look at Alessandro Allori's *Last Supper* in the next room on your way out – one of the latest Florentine renditions of this subject, painted in 1584.

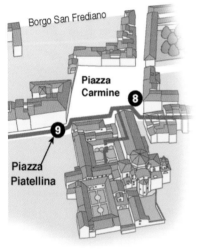

9 Leave the church and turn left, entering **Piazza Piatellina**. On the right, at **no. 9**, is **Hemingway**, serving decadently rich hot chocolate and a vintage cocktail list. Continue on to **Via dell'Orto**, savouring the peace of the neighbourhood. There are a number of eateries on this street, the best being **Il Guscio** at **no. 49**.

The old city walls of San Frediano.

10 At the end of this street turn right down **Viale Ludovico Ariosto**, which hugs the wall of the **Jewish Cemetery**. Straight ahead you'll see **Porta San Frediano**, one of the five old *portas* to be found in Oltrarno (next to it, a marble slab shows the height of the Arno when it flooded in 1966). Beyond the *porta* you'll find **Trattoria Sabotino** cosily wedged into the corner of **Via Pisana** (**no. 2**). Often labelled as 'authentic' by locals, this is a cheap and cheerful restaurant with plenty of atmosphere, but don't expect fine dining. From here, head down **Borgo San Frediano**, lined with a heady mix of trendy new bars and working-class artisans. Be sure to have a wander through **Galleria Romanelli** at **no. 70**, a sculpture studio stacked with unique pieces, from busts to equestrian monuments, before continuing down **Borgo San Frediano**.

The organ in San Frediano in Cestello.

⓫ Dip down **Via di Cestello** to take a look at **San Frediano in Cestello**, a Baroque Roman Catholic church with a light and breezy blue and white interior. Then retrace your steps to **Borgo San Frediano** and continue left until you find yourself back in the capacious **Piazza del Carmine**, the plain façade of its *chiesa* staring at you from the other side. This *piazza* has managed to retain a local and authentic feel when compared with its more party-centric neighbour, Santo Spirito. On your right, **Trattoria del Carmine (no. 33)** is charming spot to eat if you want to feel like a local, while **Trattoria Napoleone** on the left (**no. 24**) is a great pizzeria, with a separate menu devoted to the Tuscan delicacy *tartufo* (both of these are recommended in our itinerary for **La Dolce Vita**, page 84).

⓬ **Borgo San Frediano** will merge into **Via Santo Spirito**, equally awash with artisan workshops. Gems include **Maurizio and Salici** at **no. 32** with an enticing warren of antiques and **Castorina** (open since 1895) at **no. 15**, which sells hand-made wooden objects specially treated to give them an antique finish. The print shop **L'Ippogriffo Stampe D'arte** at **no. 5** belongs to Gianni and Duccio Rafaelli, two of the last master etchers in the city. They use techniques passed down in their families over the past 500 years, and often spend up to two months engraving one copper plate. Delicious eateries are also plentiful on this stretch. Some of the best include **Il Santo Bevitore** (**no. 36**) along with its cosy neighbouring wine bar **Il Santino**. **Trattoria L'Angiolino's** (**no. 10**) is a great place for sharing a bloody plate of *bistecca fiorentina*.

--Sunburst ornament from Castorina.

The interior of Castorina.

An etching in L'Ippogriffo Stampe D'Arte.

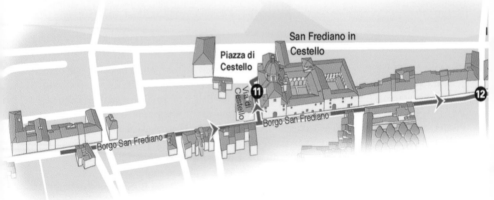

A window box on Via Santo Spirito.

⓭ Cross **Via Maggio** and bear right down **Via dello Sprone**, which takes you to **Piazza della Passera**. There are two versions of the story as to how this little *piazza* acquired its name (given officially in 2005, but used in practice for many years previously). One tells of a group of children who failed to save a dying sparrow they found here (*passera* is Italian for sparrow), its death causing the Black Death of 1348 that killed half a city. Another more accepted and less grisly version is that a number of brothels used to be located here (*passera* is also slang for genitalia). Today you'd hardly guess at the tranquil square's chequered history: it's home to **4Leoni**, famous for its pear ravioli, and **Gelateria della Passera**, widely considered to serve the best *gelato* in Florence (their *gelato di cocco* is sensational).

⓮ Continue down **Via dello Sprone**, with **Ditta Artigianale** on the right at **no. 5**, a trendy café serving artisan coffee and delectable pistachio cream croissants. This will take you back on to **Via de Guicciardini**, where you turn left, back towards the **Ponte Vecchio**.

Clockwise from the left: decorative radish plant; croissants from Ditta Artigianale; a painted putto from Castorina.

Street art in Oltrarno.

ENDS

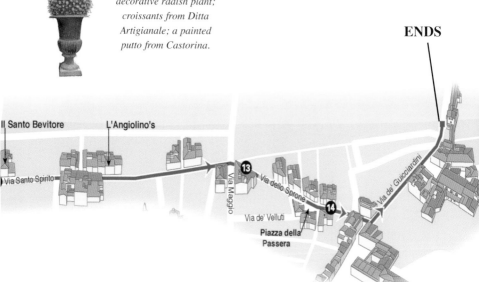

The Boboli Gardens: A Bucolic Ramble

The Boboli is the ultimate Italianate garden. Its original design was laid out by Niccolò 'Il Tribolo' in 1549 when the land was bought by the Medici family, but its appearance and design are equally the result of four centuries of Il Tribolo's artistic successors. Having exclusively been the playground of nobles, changing hands between various grand duchies, today the Boboli opens its arms to the public as a green oasis of calm, offering Florentines respite from the steamy summer months. The route makes a charming break from the typical Florentine fare of churches and *palazzi*, so pack a picnic (and lots of water – there's no café), and expect a soothing stroll through cypresses and citrus groves, evergreen copses and espaliered hedges, with remarkable sculptures at every turn.

The Kaffeehaus.

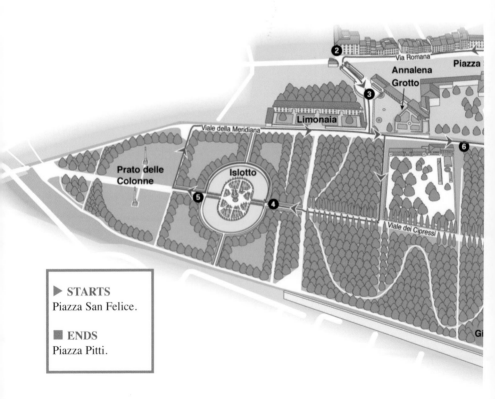

▶ **STARTS**
Piazza San Felice.

■ **ENDS**
Piazza Pitti.

Also expect to be stimulated, because the Boboli recently earned the designation of open-air museum: its gardens, monuments and vast collection of sculptures combine to make it a walkable masterpiece, but its size and layout means it's easy to miss some of the greatest attractions. This walk ensures you see all the highlights (and much more), taking you down Via Romana to the Annalena entrance, unknown to most tourists, and meandering through the gardens back towards the Pitti Palace.

View of the Palazzo Pitti, as seen from the Neptune Fountain. Below, flowers.

STARTS **ENDS**

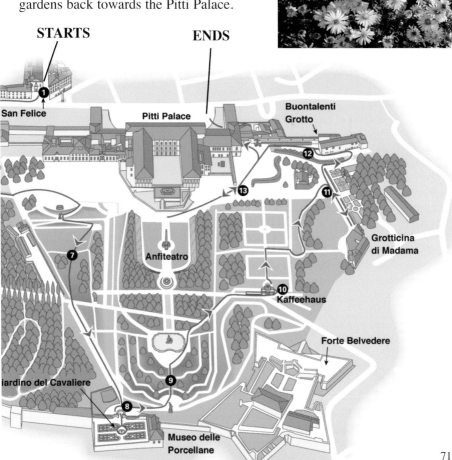

THE BOBOLI GARDENS: A BUCOLIC RAMBLE

Colonna di San Felice.

❶ Begin in **Piazza San Felice**, facing the 15thC Michelozzian façade of **Chiesa San Felice** (containing a gilded *Crucifix* attributed to the Gothic master, Giotto). Across the square you will see the **Colonna di San Felice**, erected by Cosimo I in 1572 to symbolize the victorious Battle of Marciano. Bear left down **Via Romana**, the oldest and longest road in Oltrarno, which leads up to the old trade gateway of Porta Romana. In centuries past, this road was frequented by hundreds of dignitaries, travellers and pilgrims coming to and from Rome. Nowadays it's home to numerous artisan workspaces and shops, but the road's buildings bear testament to its antique pedigree. Look out for **La Specola** very soon on your right (**no. 17**). This is not only the oldest part of the **Museum of Natural History** (which has branches across Florence) but the oldest museum in all of Europe, originally housing Cosimo Medici's collection. A worthy stop for science and history lovers, it now houses the zoological collection, including a room of wax anatomical models that comes with a warning sign for the squeamish.

The ancient road of Via Romana.

❷ About half way down this road the **Annalena entrance** will appear on your left. (If you haven't already got a picnic, **Panificio La Favola** a little further ahead at **no. 77** serves takeaway *panini*). The entrance was built in 1815, intended as Grand Duke Leopoldo II's gateway to the **Limonaia**. Nowadays it caters for savvy Italian locals wishing to avoid the queues outside the Pitti Palace. Once you've bought a ticket head into the entrance courtyard and you will see the **Annalena Grotto** straight ahead. Grottoes (natural caves found near water) were romanticized and reproduced artificially in Italy from the 16thC onwards, following classical examples. When this particular grotto was designed in 1817, *Adam & Eve* (carved in 1616) was pinched from the Viale dei Cipressi to be placed here, against a cavernous backdrop dripping in stalactites (icicle-like formations found on the walls of grottoes), inlaid with shells rich in mother-of-pearl. The ceiling is decorated with blue panels bearing the attributes of oceanic gods.

Viale della Meridiana

Islotto

The wisteria-clad Annalena entrance.

❸ From the Grotto go up the hill to exit the entrance courtyard, turning left, and then immediate right down a narrow lane flanked by tall hedges. This leads you to the magnificent **Viale dei Cipressi**, where you turn right. Also known as **'Il Viottolone'** (meaning 'large path') its construction begun in 1612 – the year the cypress trees were planted – as part of Grand Duke Cosimo de Medici II's early 17thC expansion of the garden. It was designed as the central axis of the garden, connecting the labyrinth at its southern end (destroyed in 1834) to the marvellous **Vasca dell'Isola** (Island Pond), which you will see looming towards you at the end of the path.

Adam & Eve *in the Annalena Grotto.*

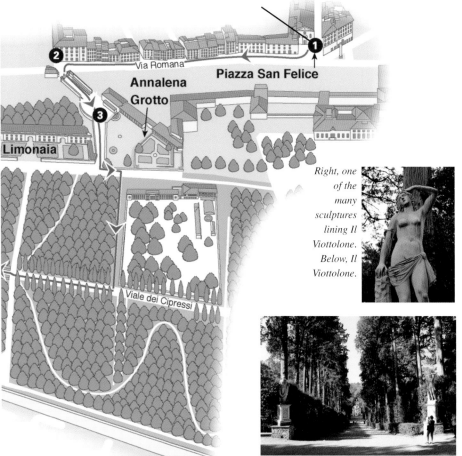

STARTS

Via Romana

Piazza San Felice

Annalena Grotto

Limonaia

Viale dei Cipressi

Right, one of the many sculptures lining Il Viottolone. Below, Il Viottolone.

❹ Emerge into **Piazzale dell'Isola** which encircles the **Isolotto**, a large oval basin with an island at its centre, designed by Giulio Parigi in 1612 by the order of Cosimo de Medici II. The Isolotto was originally conceived as a garden for the cultivation of citrus fruits – the archetypically Italian fruit of which the Medici were especially enamoured – and in summer it continues to brim over with nearly 200 potted citrus plants, which are kept snug in the greenhouses during winter. Its centrepiece is Giambologna's 17thC *Fontana dell'Oceano*, a muscular Neptune under which crouch three figures representing the Great Rivers: Ganges, Nile and Eurphrates. The whole sculptural group is perched on a basin made out of a huge slab of granite Cosimo imported from Elba to be brought here. The square itself is lined with espalier hedges and niches containing a variety of 17thC statues depicting peasants and hunters: resounding subjects throughout the garden, because they were believed to suit its bucolic atmosphere. At the back you'll find *Perseus on Horseback* erupting from the water's crystalline surface.

The Isolotto.

Pegasus, in front of the Meridian wing of the courtyard.

A Roman bust in Prato delle Colonne.

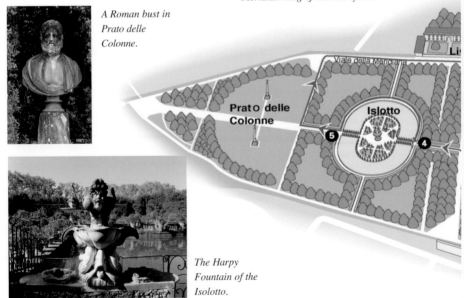

The Harpy Fountain of the Isolotto.

❺ Continue beyond the Isolotto on the path parallel to Il Vottolone and you emerge into the **Prato delle Colonne** (Meadow of Columns), a semicircular lawn featuring two porphyry columns and twelve colossal busts wedged into its hedges (some of which are Roman originals). Take a right as you enter and turn right again down **Viale della Meridiana**, and you'll see the **Limonaia** on your left just before the Annalena entrance. This building, along with the Kaffeehaus and

The Limonaia.

Meridian Building, is an 18thC addition by the Habsburg-Lorraine's, who were ushered into power when Gian Gastone de'Medici died in 1737 and ended the three-century tenure of Medici rule. Now the pastel-grey Limonaia continues to serve its original purpose as a glorified greenhouse, housing over 500 potted citrus plants.

❻ Continue along this path, going all the way up the hill, and you will emerge into a large courtyard belonging to the **Meridian wing** of the **Pitti Palace**. A Hapsburg-Lorraine addition from the 18thC, it now houses one of the world's most comprehensive **Costume Museums**. Head up the ramps opposite the wing that lead past a giant Roman bath and sculpture of Pegasus, which will take you to the **Chestnut Grove**. This is an ideal spot to tuck into your picnic beneath the shade of the trees, whilst looking across the top of the Pitti Palace at the splendiferous view of the city's fabled domes, fading into the blue Tuscan hills beyond.

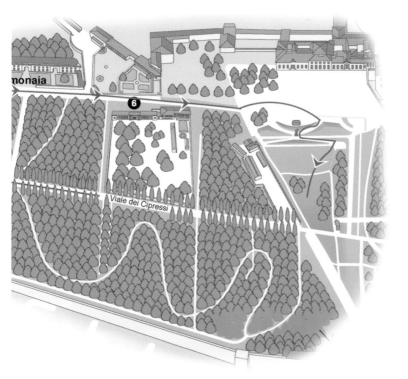

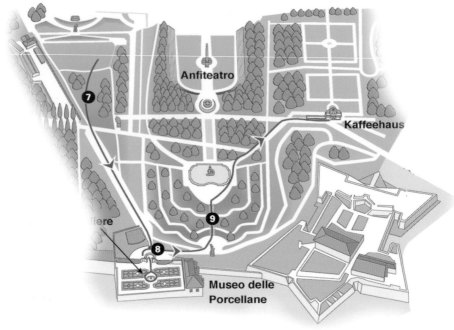

Monkey statues on the fountain of Giardino del Cavaliere.

The Porcelain Museum.

❼ Once you're replenished, head straight across the **Chestnut Grove** (which features a giant sculpture of a face and ancient column) past a row of houses on your right (where there's a **WC**). Keep going in this direction and you will come to an elegant Rococo double-staircase, designed by Giuseppe del Rosso in 1729. Ascend the stairs, past the sculptural *Muses*, and you arrive into **Giardino del Cavaliere** – the highest point of the Boboli, offering an enchanting view of the Florentine hills. The partitioned garden, originally intended for medicinal plants, now brims with fragrant roses, all of which are in bloom in May. The building, previously a Knight's Lodge, now houses a rather lovely **Porcelain Museum**.

8 Come back down the steps and bear right down a path that will lead you to the colossal sculpture of *Abundance*, recognized by the sheaf of wheat and cornucopia she holds in her hands. This sculpture (begun by Giambologna in 1608) was first intended as a portrait of Giovanna of Austria to stand on a column in Piazza San Marco, but when it was relocated here in 1636 it became an allegorical representation of the Tuscan state. This is an ideal standpoint from which to appreciate the axis that begins with the **Antifeatro**, up to the *Neptune Fountain* and resting on *Abundance* – the deliberate end point of these three tiers.

9 Head down the steps straight ahead to take a closer look at the *Neptune Fountain*, affectionately nicknamed '**The Fork**' by Florentines because it depicts Neptune brandishing his trident off a cliff edge. There will be an opportunity at the end of the walk to explore the Antifeatro, but for now bear right around the edge of Neptune's basin and take the narrow path in the corner, flanked by two espalier hedges. Continue down this path and the mint-and-white **Kaffeehaus** will crest at the top, like a beautifully iced Rococo cake. Like the Limonaia this was designed by Zanobi del Rosso, intended as a resting place for fatigued courtiers as they explored the gardens.

The Kaffeehaus.

View of the Tuscan hills from Giardino del Cavaliere. Below, the Neptune Fountain.

Abundance.

THE BOBOLI GARDENS: A BUCOLIC RAMBLE

⑩ Descend the stairs to the partitioned garden below to view the façade in all its splendour, before turning right at the central gravel path (before the garden with the sculpture of *Ganymede* astride an eagle) and all the way down the tree-lined path, which will take you into a small courtyard, across which is a partitioned garden with a statue of *Jupiter* in it. Turn right along the gate – at the end of this path will be the **Grotticina di Madama**, the oldest of the Boboli Grottoes.

Palazzo Pitti, as seen from the Anfiteatro.

Ganymede.

⑪ Retrace your steps past *Jupiter* and you will see a hedge-lined path on your right which will take you to the **Grotto Buontalenti**. This enormous surrealistic grotto (probably the most famous in Europe) is decorated inside and out with stalactites. It used to be the home of Michelangelo's famous sculpture *Prisoners* (now in the Accademia) and still exhibits a number of Mannerist sculptures. The first of its three-part interior is frescoed with a bucolic menagerie of woodland creatures, designed to make you feel you're in a natural grotto sheltering shepherds. Walk through the caverns of the grotto to look at *Paris and Helen* by Vincenzo de Rossi, followed by Giambologna's *Bathing Venus* in its third and final room.

Grotto Buontalenti.

Morgante the dwarf.

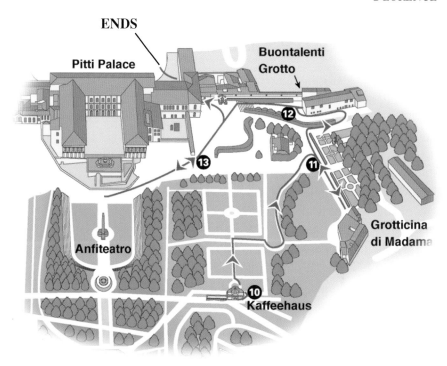

ENDS

Pitti Palace

Buontalenti Grotto

12

13

11

Grotticina di Madama

Anfiteatro

10
Kaffeehaus

⓬ Exit the grotto, ascending the steps straight ahead to **Bacchus Square**, named for the sculpture of the fat dwarf astride a turtle, erroneously known as Bacchus (he in fact represents the dwarf Morgante, who was an entertainer at Grand Duke Cosimo I court). Before taking the exit through the **Pitti Palace** straight ahead, bear left, walking around the edge of the Pitti Palace until you reach the **Anfiteatro**, with the colossal Roman bath and Egyptian obelisk. Aside from giving you a view of the 24 statues surrounding the theatre, you also have a more precipitous perspective of the axis leading up past the *Neptune Fountain* to *Abundance*.

⓭ Retrace your steps to **Bacchus Square**, waving to Morgante before departing through the arch – and preferably heading for a glass of *rosso* and *apertivo* in **Piazza Santo Spirito**, just around the corner.

Palazzo Pitti.

La Dolce Vita:
An Evening Itinerary

La dolce vita. That inimitably sweet quality of the Italian lifestyle, hard to define yet indisputably a product of Italy's culture, weather, pace of life, and (perhaps most important in Florence) food and drink – especially the use of local ingredients enjoyed with a glug or three of Italian wine.

Basilica di Santo Spirito at dusk.

More of an evening itinerary than a walk, this route is devoted to the good life in Florence. It's by no means prescriptive: pitch your tent for the night if you're having too much fun to move on, and save later suggestions for another evening. Most important, take your time. Italians aren't for trudging doggedly from one bar to another,

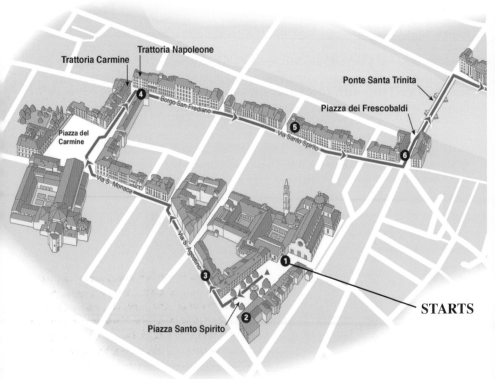

but slowly savouring the ebb and flow of an evening, oscillating between drinks and food, action and repose. While exploring traditional venues, the walk is also a celebration of the city's nightlife, for which Florence has become something of a European hotspot.

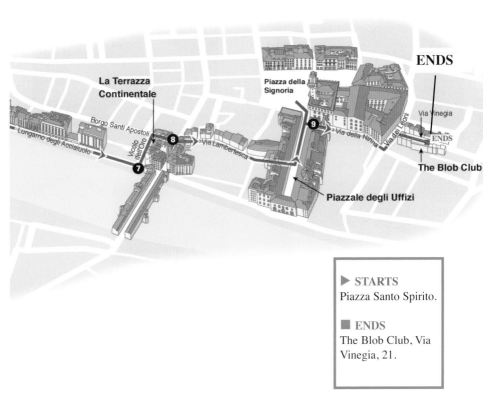

The Arno by night.

The route takes in trendy bars and authentic restaurants in Oltrarno (we will suggest two *trattorias* for dinner, both in Piazza del Carmine – take your pick and book ahead); a moonlit stroll across the river, with several bars and a *gelateria* along the way, finally ending up at The Blob Club – ungraciously named, but buckets of fun.

ENDS

La Terrazza
Continentale

Piazza della
Signoria

Via Vinegia

Borgo Santi Apostoli

Lungarno degli Acciaiuolo

Vicolo dell'Oro

Via Lambertesca

Via della Ninna

Via dei Leoni

ENDS

8

7

9

The Blob Club

Piazzale degli Uffizi

▶ **STARTS**
Piazza Santo Spirito.

■ **ENDS**
The Blob Club, Via Vinegia, 21.

81

La Dolce Vita: An Evening Itinerary

❶ There's nowhere better for observing the permutations of daily life in Florence than **Piazza Santo Spirito** – undoubtedly the beating heart of Oltrarno. Sit outside for the day and you'll see the daily food market setting up its wares, with the influx from lunch followed by the lull of siesta time, all building towards fiesta time – beginning around 7pm when crowds gather for *aperitivo*. This supremely civilized custom (happening between 7pm and 9pm) is not, as sometimes practised by tourists, meant to substitute dinner,

The bar at Cabiria.

but to stimulate, or *open*, your appetite beforehand (*aperitivo* derives from the Latin *aperire*, meaning 'to open'). The many bars around the *piazza* all have their *raison d'être*, but for an *aperitivo*, take a seat outside **Volume** (**no. 5**), the trendy 'industrial' themed bar that brings a tray of snacks such as olives, *focaccia* and dip, with your *aperol spritz* (the traditional *apertif* cocktail). Or, if you're restrained enough, head to **Tamero** (**no. 18**). Their buffet-style *aperitivo* includes heartier dishes such as ragu pasta and aubergine parmigiana. Alternatively, buy a takeaway cocktail (**Carbiria's** Bloody Mary is a winner) to drink in the square (on any given night you'll see swathes of people drinking on the church steps – a divisive practice, for obvious reasons).

The exterior of Palazzo Guadagni.

Aperitivo at Tamero.

The terrace of Palazzo Guadagni at dusk.

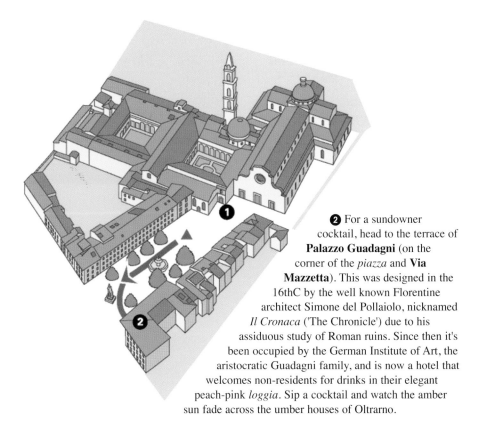

2 For a sundowner cocktail, head to the terrace of **Palazzo Guadagni** (on the corner of the *piazza* and **Via Mazzetta**). This was designed in the 16thC by the well known Florentine architect Simone del Pollaiolo, nicknamed *Il Cronaca* ('The Chronicle') due to his assiduous study of Roman ruins. Since then it's been occupied by the German Institute of Art, the aristocratic Guadagni family, and is now a hotel that welcomes non-residents for drinks in their elegant peach-pink *loggia*. Sip a cocktail and watch the amber sun fade across the umber houses of Oltrarno.

Palazzo Guadagni at nightfall.

❸ Ten minutes before your dinner reservation, head down **Via S. Agostino** at the corner of the *piazza*, and continue in the same direction down **Via Santa Monaca**. You'll emerge into **Piazza del Carmine**. Two possibilities for dinner are located across the square. **Trattoria Carmine (no. 18)** is ideal for traditionalists who want to be surrounded by locals. Here you can choose to dine under the stars while eating local dishes such as *bistecca alla fiorentina*. **Trattoria Napoleone (no. 24)** is a marvellous pizzeria with a separate menu devoted entirely to the Tuscan delicacy *tartufo* (truffle). Its bedizened interior and mood lighting (with private rooms for groups) is an ideal prelude for a night on the razz.

The mixologist at work in MAD.

Mood lighting and drinks at Trattoria Napoleone.

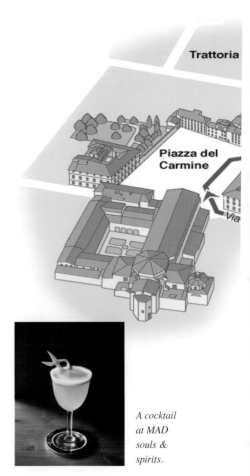

❹ End dinner with a *limoncello* (the traditional lemon-flavoured *digestivo*) and begin your stroll down **Borgo San Frediano**. San Frediano was recently hailed by *Lonely Planet* as one of the top ten 'coolest' neighbourhoods in the world, evident from the slew of trendy bars you'll pass on this street. Begin at **MAD souls and spirits (no. 36)** a few doors down from Napoleone, where bonafide mixologists serve craft cocktails to their arty clientele. **Gesto** at **no. 27** does Italian tapas with cocktails, while **Kawaii** at **no. 8** – a Japanese fusion bar – makes sake-based cocktails.

A cocktail at MAD souls & spirits.

5 If you're looking for somewhere a little more authentic, you'll find **Il Santino** on your left, once **Borgo San Frediano** merges onto **Via Santo Spirito**. This quaint and cosy wine bar is attached to the hugely popular restaurant, **Il Santo Bevitore (no. 66)**. Further along you'll see **Trattoria Angiolino (no. 36)**, an old favourite among many in the area, and especially good for Tuscan classics such as *pappa al pomodoro* and *ribollita*.

Inside Trattoria Angiolino.

Mural depicting the good life in Trattoria Angiolino.

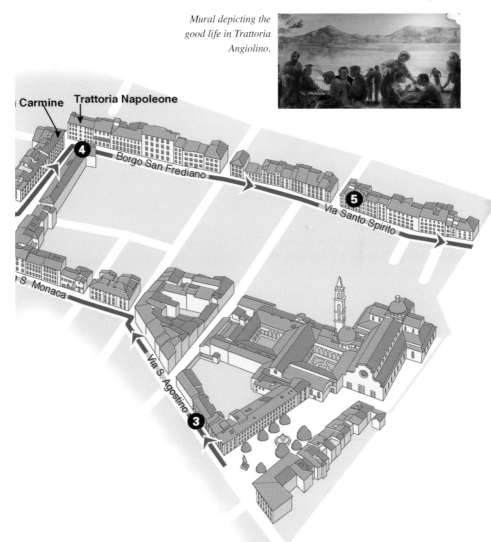

View of the Ponte Vecchio from Ponte Santa Trinita.   *A riverside walk.*

6 Take a left at **Piazza dei Frescobaldi**, and (if you have room for dessert) purchase a *gelato* at **Gelateria Santa Trinita (no. 8)**. Black Sesame flavour is their unusual but highly popular speciality. Then proceed across **Ponte Santa Trinita**, pausing halfway to admire the spectacular view of the Ponte Vecchio reflected in the glittering Arno. At the end of the bridge turn right down **Lungarno degli Acciaiuoli** for a riverside stroll, savouring the beauty of Florence by night.

7 Turn left at **Vicolo dell'Oro**. On the right, at **no. 6**, you'll see **La Terrazza Continentale**, which has a roof-top bar (open until 11pm) and a panoramic view. Pop upstairs for another cocktail-with-a-view, this time across to the city's hallowed dome, illuminated at night.

8 At the end of **Vicolo dell'Oro** turn right down **Borgo Sant'Apostoli**, and continue in the same direction as the street merges on to **Via Lambertesca**, passing several bars. This takes you to **Piazzale degli Uffizi**. Turn left and continue into **Piazza della Signoria**, which is resplendent at night, when

moonlight dances off its marble inhabitants. Until fairly recently the *popolo* of Florence believed the city's statues were possessed by spirits, and that Ammannati's *Neptune* imprisoned the mighty god of the Arno. When the moon shone on him at midnight, so the story goes, he came to life and conversed with other sculptures in the square.

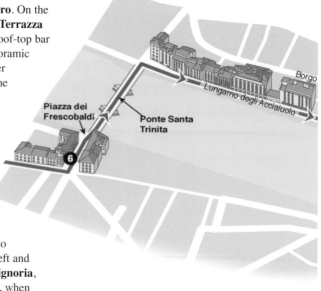

Above, the Loggiato degli Uffizi. Left, the Palazzo Vecchio.

9 Leave the *piazza* the way you came, turning left down **Via della Ninna**. Take the first left down **Via dei Leoni**, then first right down **Via Vinegia**. **The Blob Club** will appear on your right at **no. 21** (easy to miss as the front doors are soundproof and unassuming in appearance). In many ways a generic club, this might seem an odd choice, but as the go-to for Florentines and tourists alike, it's a rite of passage for any stay in the city. There's a swinging dance floor and a 'chill' area upstairs.

If Blob doesn't take your fancy, there are plenty of options further east in the lively Santa Croce neighbourhood. A few suggestions include **Dondino**, a rustic wine bar in the **Piazza Santa Croce** (**no. 6**) in view of the lovely church façade; **Beer House Club** (**Corso dei Tintori, 34**), which serves artisan beers in a relaxed sitting; and **FUK** on **Via Giuseppe, 19**, with an excellent cocktail menu. All four are open until late.

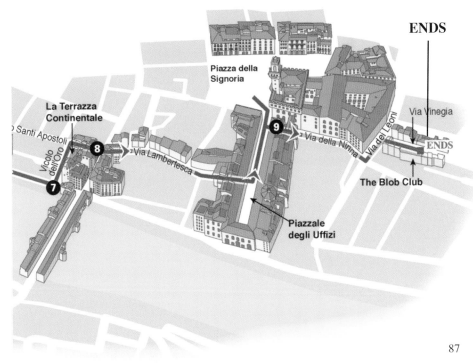

Into the Heights: San Miniato al Monte

This magical trail explores the hilly area to the south-east of the Arno, beyond the crumbling city walls that hem in the Historic Centre. Not your usual litany of *palazzi* and churches (though they certainly feature), this walk stands out for both variety and breathtaking beauty – and despite being a route less travelled by tourists, it could well be the highlight of your visit to the city. The walk begins by taking you through the traditional artisan neighbourhood of San Niccoló, then up through an idyllic rose garden to Piazzale Michelangelo, with its celebrated panoramic view. The crowning glory of the walk is San Miniato al Monte, situated on one of the

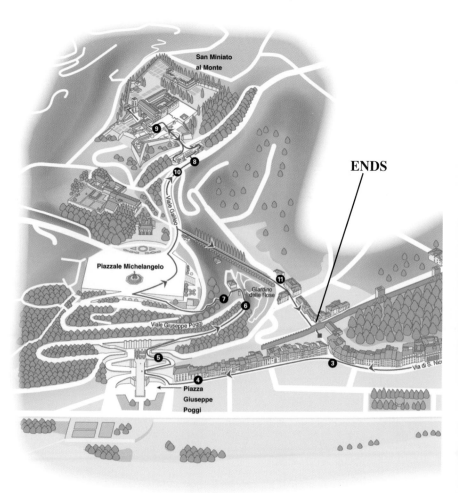

highest points in Florence. This 10,000-year-old purveyor of the 'flourishing town' is one of the most beautiful Romanesque churches in all of Tuscany, with a wonderful 19thC cemetery in its backyard.

When you reach the finishing point at Porta San Miniato you could easily go on to do **Off the Beaten Track** (page 96) in reverse, as the walks are closely related and share the same end point. This is recommended if you have limited time in Florence and want a full day of exploring the city's medieval boundaries – though brace yourself for a few steep climbs by making use of the wine bars and restaurants along the way.

Giardino delle Rose.

San Miniato al Monte.

▶ **STARTS**
Ponte alle Grazie
(Oltrarno side).

■ **ENDS**
Porta San Miniato.

STARTS

The view from Piazzale Michelangelo.

INTO THE HEIGHTS: SAN MINIATO AL MONTE

Ponte Vecchio (as seen from Ponte alle Grazie).

The painted exterior of Alessandro Dari.

❶ Begin on the Oltrarno side of **Ponte alle Grazie**. Perhaps one of the plainest of the central bridges, it nevertheless offers an excellent viewpoint from which to take a snap of its more colourful neighbour, the Ponte Vecchio. With your back to the bridge, head straight up across the narrow **Piazza de' Mozzi**. You will pass the **Museo Bardini** on your left (dip down **Via dei Renai** on your left to find the entrance at no. 36), a *palazzo* housing the eclectic collection of antiquarian dealer Stefano Bardini, which he bequeathed to the city upon his death in 1922. Continue past it, turning left into **Via di S. Niccoló**.

Inside Alessandro Dari's jewellry shop.

❷ Follow the curve of this charming Renaissance street, home to a myriad of artisans, *trattorias* and small galleries. Very soon on your right at **no. 115** you will come by the workshop of **Alessandro Dari** – the world-famous goldsmith – concealed behind the exterior of a handsomely painted 15thC *palazzo*. Wander through this Aladdin's cave of a shop to see how the Maestro has elevated this quintessentially Florentine craft to an art using Etrurian and Renaissance techniques, passed down through his family's workshop since 1603.

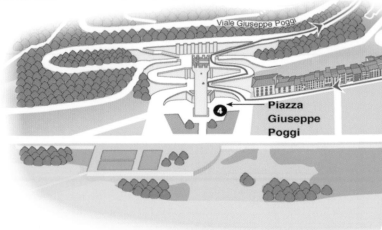

Painted palazzos on Via San Niccolo.

Torre di San Niccolo.

❸ Half-way down **Via di S. Niccoló** you will pass the **Chiesa di San Niccoló**. Originating from the 12thC, its plain façade belies a number of artistic gems inside from the likes of Pollaiolo, Michelozzo and Neri di Bicci. The **Piazza San Niccoló** in which it resides hosts a number of eateries: head to **Il Rifrullo** for excellent *aperitivo* and **Osteria Antica Mescita** for typical Tuscan fare. The square's atmosphere is chilled in the daytime, awaiting a more buzzing night-time ambience.

Torre di San Niccolo.

❹ Continue to the end of this street and the **Torre di San Niccoló** will loom at the end – as though this winding street were transporting you gradually toward the medieval beginnings of Florence that are celebrated in rest of the walk. Pause at **Stefano Berner (no. 2)**, renowned seller of classy bespoke leather shoes. You'll emerge into **Piazza Giuseppe Poggi**, dominated by the **Torre di San Niccoló**. Despite its name, this is the remains of one of the many medieval *portas* leading out of the city walls.

STARTS

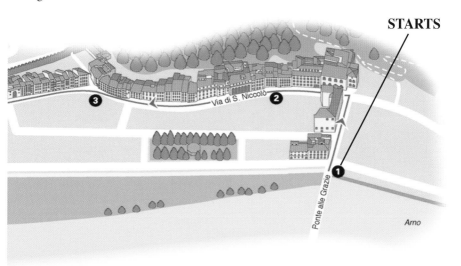

INTO THE HEIGHTS: SAN MINIATO AL MONTE

5 Ascend what are known as the 'Poggi ramps' (named for their 19thC architect, Giuseppe Poggi) behind the tower. On the first level you're confronted with five colossal arches concealing surrealistic grottoes, their walls dripping in stalactites (icicle-shaped formations) as though they've been underwater for centuries. At the top of the ramps, bear right along **Viale Giuseppe Poggi.**

The view from Piazzale Michelangelo.

One of the 350 species of rose in the Giardino delle Rose.

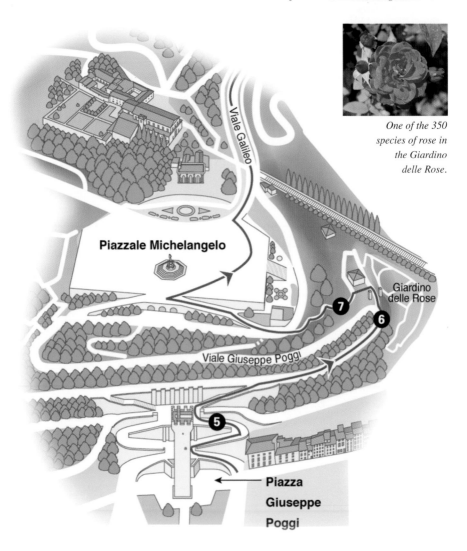

6 You will see the entrance to the **Giardino delle Rose** tucked away on the first bend in the road. This bountiful garden (open all year, 8am-8pm) grows 350 species of rose, all of which are in full bloom between May and June, and has a Japanese garden donated by Florence's twin city, Kyoto. Twelve beautiful sculptures by the Belgian artist Jean-Michel Folon are dotted among the shrubs. The garden's lower level, to the right as you enter, is an ideal place to sit and meditate on the Florentine vista before you: a terracotta city fading into blue, the crumbling city walls cascading into the green valley in your foreground.

View of the city walls, as seen from the Giardino delle Rose.

Two of the twelve sculptures donated to Florence in 2005 by Jean-Michel Folon's widow. Cast in an earthy bronze, his whimsical hybrid creatures are designed to integrate perfectly with the bucolic surroundings.

7 When you're ready, take the staircase directly to the left of where you entered the Rose Garden. This takes you to **Piazzale Michelangelo**, essentially a two-tiered balcony famous for its spectacular view of the Florentine skyline. In spite of the myth claiming it's existed since the birth of Florence itself, this *piazza* was in fact a fairly late addition, designed by Giuseppe Poggi in 1869 as part of a plan to restructure the city walls. Aside from a

The bronze replica of Michelangelo's David in Piazzale Michelangelo.

replica bronze David, the wonders of the *piazza* extend outwards rather than inwards – there is little to see beyond the stupendous view (which is quite enough). Once you've taken a snap alongside the other hoards of tourists, cross the square and bear right up **Viale Galileo**, passing the **Chiesa di San Salvatore al Monte** and a **WC** on your left as you go.

Chiesa di San Salvatore al Monte.

INTO THE HEIGHTS: SAN MINIATO AL MONTE

8 You'll arrive at a double staircase on your left, which will take you up to **San Miniato al Monte**, the 1,000-year-old monastery named for the obscure patron saint of Florence, San Minius. Revered as the city's first Christian martyr, legend claims that this Armenian soldier was decapitated by the Romans on the shores of the Arno in 250AD, after which he duly picked up his head and climbed this hill to be buried. In 1018 the Florentine Archbishop Hildebrand constructed the church

San Miniato al Monte.

anew in its Romanesque style to house the bones of this martyr, and the Benedictine monks have lived here ever since. On the polychrome façade (reminiscent of the Baptistery) the words, *'This is the gate of heaven'* (Genesis 28:17) are inlaid in marble, and when you enter the magnificent interior – perhaps the loveliest in Florence – you will understand why. Among its innumerable marvels is the 'carpet of marble' inlaid with signs of the zodiac, frescoes by Spinello Aretino in the Sacristy, and an underground crypt sheltering the remains of St Minius.

A column from San Miniato, with an original capital poached from Roman ruins.

9 To the right as you leave the church is a charming gift shop selling soaps, cakes and candles hand-made by the monks, as well as the entrance to the **Cimitero delle Porte di San Miniato** (The Sacred Doors Cemetery). The notion of building a cemetary at San Miniato was first proposed in 1837, and went ahead in tandem with the urban developments of Giuseppe Poggi during this century. Initially entrusted to Niccolò Matas – the architect responsible for the rather ugly façade of Basilica di Santa Croce – the design was later handed over to Mariano Falcini in the 1860s. Falcini transformed the area surrounding the church - formerly the site of a 16thC fortress - into this extraordinarily unique cemetery. Amid hundreds of elaborate neo-medieval tombs a number of Italian luminaries are buried, including Carlo Lorenzini (the author of Pinocchio) and Vasco Pratolini (three-times winner of the Nobel Prize for Literature).

Cimitero delle Porte di San Miniato.

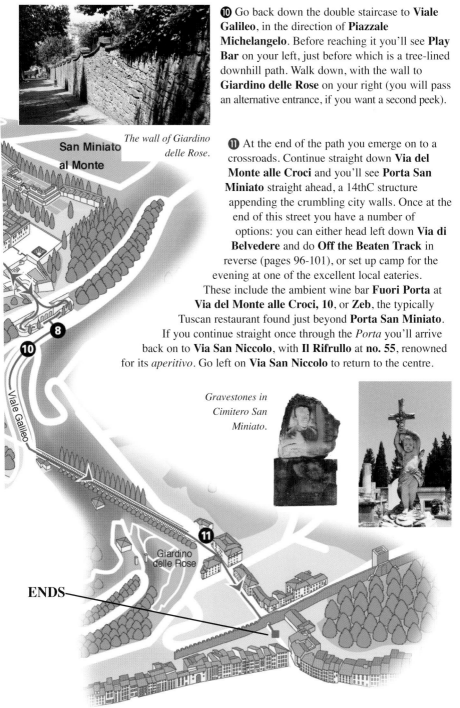

10 Go back down the double staircase to **Viale Galileo**, in the direction of **Piazzale Michelangelo**. Before reaching it you'll see **Play Bar** on your left, just before which is a tree-lined downhill path. Walk down, with the wall to **Giardino delle Rose** on your right (you will pass an alternative entrance, if you want a second peek).

The wall of Giardino delle Rose.

11 At the end of the path you emerge on to a crossroads. Continue straight down **Via del Monte alle Croci** and you'll see **Porta San Miniato** straight ahead, a 14thC structure appending the crumbling city walls. Once at the end of this street you have a number of options: you can either head left down **Via di Belvedere** and do **Off the Beaten Track** in reverse (pages 96-101), or set up camp for the evening at one of the excellent local eateries. These include the ambient wine bar **Fuori Porta** at **Via del Monte alle Croci, 10**, or **Zeb**, the typically Tuscan restaurant found just beyond **Porta San Miniato**. If you continue straight once through the *Porta* you'll arrive back on to **Via San Niccolo**, with **Il Rifrullo** at **no. 55**, renowned for its *aperitivo*. Go left on **Via San Niccolo** to return to the centre.

Gravestones in Cimitero San Miniato.

San Miniato al Monte

Viale Galileo

8

10

11

Giardino delle Rose

ENDS

Off the Beaten Track: The Medieval Boundaries of Florence

The two ancient *portas* on this walk – taking you beyond the crumbling city walls to the hills south-east of the Arno – might as well be portals through time, transporting you from the Florence's popularised Renaissance centre towards its more elusive medieval past. It shares its medieval flavour with **Into the Heights** (pages 88-95) and indeed the two can be easily merged by completing one in reverse at the shared end point of Porta San Miniato. This walk, however, is even more off the tourist grid, celebrating the medieval boundaries of Florence and its proximity to the Tuscan countryside – and should be taken at a leisurely pace (what Italians might call a *passeggiata*). Highlights include a winding (and fairly steep) ascent up Costa S. Giorgio towards the suburb of Arcetri, with its tiny Romanesque church; the Bardini Gardens, still relatively unknown despite their outstanding location; the colossal Forte di Belvedere; and a stroll down the longest surviving stretch of city walls. Taking you firmly away from the hustle and bustle of the city centre, this route traverses the boundaries between urban and rural, past and present, offering a truly unique perspective on the city.

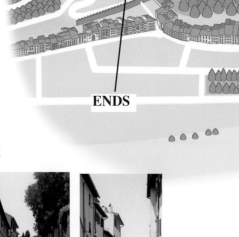

Far right, Costa S. Giorgio.
Right, Via di Belvedere.

The Wisteria Tunnel in Giardino Bardini.

The view from Forte di Belvedere.

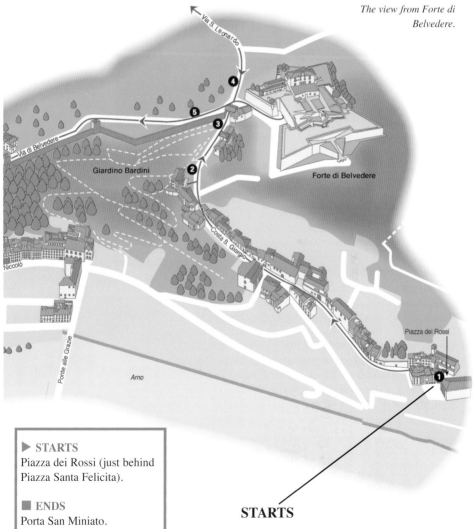

▶ **STARTS**
Piazza dei Rossi (just behind Piazza Santa Felicita).

■ **ENDS**
Porta San Miniato.

STARTS

OFF THE BEATEN TRACK: THE MEDIEVAL BOUNDARIES OF FLORENCE

❶ Begin in **Piazza dei Rossi**, just behind **Piazza Santa Felicita** and its basilica. Pop into the charming wine bar **Le Volpi e l'Uva** if you want a fortifying glass of *rosso,* before bearing right up the forked road ahead to begin your thigh-burning ascent up **Costa S. Giorgio** – a winding residential street that is perhaps one of the loveliest in Europe, leading you away from the hubbub of the centre. A vista of the Florentine skyline will appear on your left at the turning of Costa Scarpuccia. A little further ahead the **Casa di Galileo Galilei** will appear on your right at **no. 19**, distinguished by the Coats of Arms of the Galilei family (a three-rung ladder) and a portrait of Galileo above the door. The Pisan scientist lived here with his family between 1629-34 before migrating further up the hill in his old age.

Far left, view of Florence glimpsed at turning into Costa Scarpuccia. Left, vista of Costa S. Giorgio.

❷ Towards the very top of **Costa S. Giorgio** you will find the entrance to the **Bardini Villa and Gardens** on your left at **no. 2**. The gardens date all the way back to the 1200s when the land was used as a fruit orchard by the Mozzi family, but their present incarnation was largely laid out by their 19thC owner, the antiques dealer Stefano Bardini. For years after his son bequeathed them to the state they remained neglected and overgrown, before a huge restoration project saw them reopen to the public in 2000. Nearly 20 years later and the secret is barely out, and tranquility pervades. Occupying most of the steep hill rising from the Arno, the views across Florence are enchanting, as are the gardens mixed styles and myriad features, such as a huge Baroque staircase, wisteria tunnels and canals running through Anglo-Chinese gardens (bookended by an English wood to the west and Tuscan farmland to east). One could easily spend an hour ambling through the gardens and taking refreshment at its cafè.

Casa di Galileo Galilei.

Baroque staircase in Giardino Bardini.

Staircase statues in Giardino Bardini.

❸ Leave the gardens and continue to the end of **Costa S. Giorgio**. Go through the arch of **Porta S. Giorgio** – the oldest surviving *porta* in Florence, dating back to 1324 – and you'll emerge at a crossroads with the city walls on your left and the colossal wall of **Forte di Belvedere** on your right. Skirt around the fort, down **Via del Forte di S. Giorgio**, to reach the entrance. The vast star-shaped structure was designed in 1590 by Bernardo Buontalenti to protect Florence, and the reigning Medici family (who were living in yonder Palazzo Pitti) from attack. Nowadays, the fort hosts seasonal exhibitions for the public – which in the past have included the likes of Henry Moore and Anish Kapoor – and serves as a venue for elite events, such as the wedding of Kim Kardashian and Kanye West in 2014.

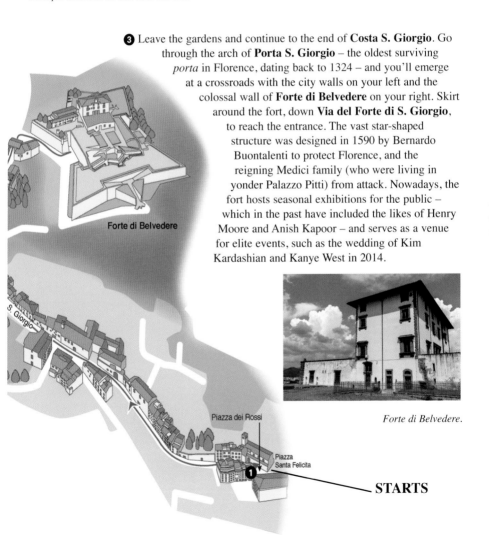

Forte di Belvedere

S. Giorgio

Piazza dei Rossi

Piazza Santa Felicita

❶

STARTS

Forte di Belvedere.

❹ Back at the crossroads of **Porta San Giorgio** head up **Via di S. Leonardo**, which takes you towards the rural suburb of Arcetri. After a four-minute walk the **Chiesa di Leonardo in Arcetri** (open 8am-12pm, and 4pm-6pm) will appear on your left at **no. 25**, perched prettily amid olive groves (the church is situated just outside the map's range). As ever with Florence, treasures are to found in the most unobtrusive places, and despite the church's modest size it's home to a marvellous marble pulpit – one that Dante and Boccaccio both lectured from in the 13thC – renowned among art historians as a masterwork of Florentine Romanesque sculpture. The church also holds three paintings by Neri di Bicci, and a lovely mosaic (on the exterior lunette) of *St Leonardo Between Two Angels*, made by Giuseppe Castellucci in 1928. If you were to continue to the top of Via di S. Leonardo you'd see a number of plaques to its illustrious past inhabitants – including Tchaikovsky and the painter Ottone Rosai – but seeing as none of these are open to the public, retrace your steps to **Porta San Giorgio**.

Porta S. Giorgio.

Far left, exterior of San Leonardo in Arcetri.
Left, lunette mosaic of St Leonardo Between Two Angels *by Giuseppe Castelucci, 1928.*

❺ Once back at the crossroads of **Porta San Giorgio** go left down **Via di Belvedere**, tracing the longest surviving stretch of the city walls. As you walk the length of this old road, listen to the birds twitter and the cicadas chirp, savouring the sense of being on the original threshold of Florence, its 14thC walls to your left and the rolling Tuscan countryside on your right.

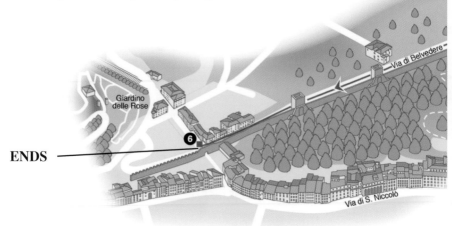

ENDS

6 At the end of **Via di Belvedere** you'll emerge on to **Via del Monte alle Croci**, with the **Porta San Miniato** on your left. At this point, the route converges with that of **Into the Heights**, so if you wish to combine the two then continue upwards past **Giardino delle Rose** to reach **San Miniato al Monte**. Alternatively, this cross-hatch of the San Niccoló neighbourhood has some of the most authentic restaurants in Florence. To the right, a little further up **Via del Monte alle Croci**, is **Fuori Porta**, a traditional wine bar serving delectable Tuscan dishes, and to the left through **Porta S. Miniato** is **Zeb** (**Via San Miniato, 2**) – a traditional deli-diner with daily specials cooked up daily by Mamma Giuseppina. **Via San Miniato** takes you back on to **Via di. San Niccoló**, with yet more *aperitivo* and *cena* stops to choose from, such as **Il Rifrullo** (**no. 55**) and **Cent'Ori** (**no. 48** – try the *Burrata* with shaved truffle). Head west on **Via S. Niccoló** to return to central Oltrarno.

Via di Belvedere and the 14thC city walls.

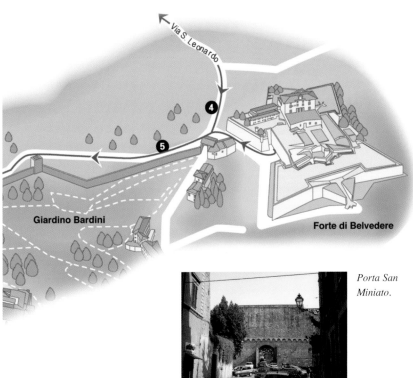

Giardino Bardini

Forte di Belvedere

Porta San Miniato.

A Hill with a View: Bellosguardo

This oft-ignored scenic walk to the sleepy hilltop of Bellosguardo –
literally meaning 'beautiful view' – is well worth the climb. Living up to
its name, this tiny hamlet offers up a view which 19thC novelist Henry
James dubbed 'the most beautiful in the world', and one that is famous (to
those in-the-know) for offering a particularly unique perspective of the city's
churches. Along the way you will embark upon a literary pilgrimage of
sorts, following in the footsteps of a number of mainstream American expat
authors who stayed here during the 19thC, including Henry James,
Nathaniel Hawthorne and Mark Twain. It was also once the part-time home

▶ STARTS
Piazza della Calza,
next to Porta Romana.

■ ENDS
Piazza Torquato Tasso.

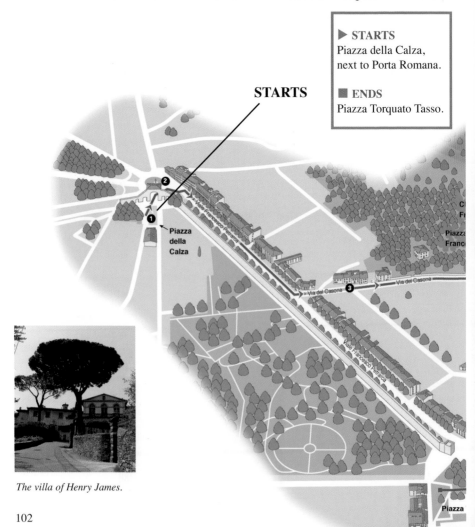

STARTS

Piazza
della
Calza

Via del Casone

Via del Casone

Via Francesco Petrarca

Piazza
Franc

Piazza

The villa of Henry James.

of astronomer Galileo Galilei, and the birthplace of Florence Nightingale.

You will begin at Porta Romana, the ancient gateway to the city, before climbing up Via di Bellosguardo to reach the top of the hill. No walk better illustrates the unique closeness of Florence to its surrounding countryside – within ten minutes you will have only the twittering of birdsong and fragrant Tuscan air for company – and not a tourist or shop in sight. On the way back you will wind up in Oltrarno's Piazza Torquato Tasso with an array of delicious eateries to choose from, as well as what we think is some of the best *gelato* in the city.

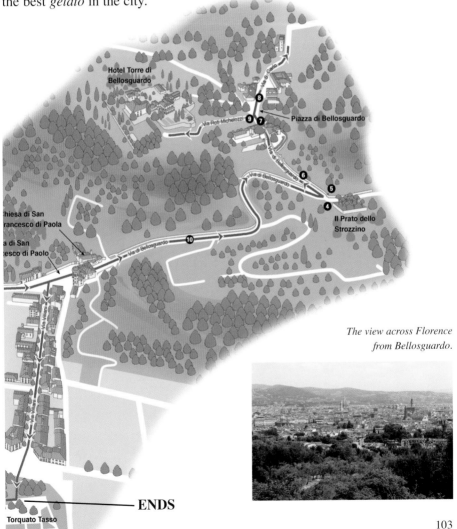

The view across Florence from Bellosguardo.

A Hill with a View: Bellosguardo

❶ Begin in **Piazza della Calza** (reached by walking to the end of **Via Romana** from **Piazza San Felice**). Above **Bar D'Angelo** you will see *La Vita di Firenze nei Secoli* ('The Life of Florence Through the Centuries') – a fresco painted by Florentine painter Mario Romoli in 1954 depicting all the heavyweights of Florentine history, from Dante to La Pira. This was painted after its Renaissance predecessor was destroyed in the Second World War.

Mario Romoli's fresco, 'La Vita di Firenze nei Secoli'.

❷ Head through the **Porta Romana** arch and you find yourself at a confluence of roads, including the southerly road pointing to Rome, which has been transporting pilgrims and dignitaries to and from this city for centuries past. Bear right down **Via Francesco Petrarco**, the tree-lined *viale* that follows the length of the now-crumbled city walls.

Porta Romana.

❸ Take the second left down **Via Del Casone** and you will emerge into **Piazza di San Francesco di Paolo**. Straight ahead to the left is **Chiesa di San Francesco di Paola**, (once the abode of the 19thC German sculptor Adolf von Hildebrand), and to the right a handsome red villa. Take the road between these two buildings, **Via di Bellosguardo**, and disarmingly soon you find yourself immersed in the Italian countryside, with wrought-iron villa gates appearing intermittently on your right.

Chiesa di San Francesco di Paola.

STARTS

Piazza della Calza

Viale Francesco Petrarco

Via del Casone

'The Sacrifice of Salvo d'Acquisto' in Prato dello Strozzino.

④ At the third bend in this rustic road you will see **Il Prato dello Strozzino** park, named for a small branch of the noble Strozzi family who once owned this land and the villa beyond. Whilst the lack of upkeep slightly eclipses the park's charm, this is still a tranquil and shady spot to take a rest before continuing your climb. The monument at the centre of the park (sculpted by Maestro Belargues) depicts *The Sacrifice of Salvo d'Acquisto*, alluding to the 20thC martyr – a young *carabiniere* who during the Second World War for saving a group of civilians from the Nazis, an act of bravery for which he was killed by German troops.

The tabernacle erected by Grand Duke Leopoldo II.

⑤ Note the tabernacle of the *Madonna & Child* on the corner of **Via di Bellosguardo** and **Via di S. Vito**, opposite the park. While these tabernacles are two-a-penny in Florence (you will pass several on this walk alone) this one comes with a rather interesting piece of history, alluding to an obscure miracle involving Grand Duke Leopoldo II of Lorraine, the mid-19thC ruler popular with Florentines because of his social conscience and shock of blond hair. In 1848, Leopoldo and his two daughters were riding along this crossroads when their horses became agitated and the carriage overturned, flinging them out. Miraculously they survived unscathed, and to show his thanks Leopoldo donated a chalice to the local parish church, and erected this tabernacle, which reads: *For grace received from a father with two daughters.*

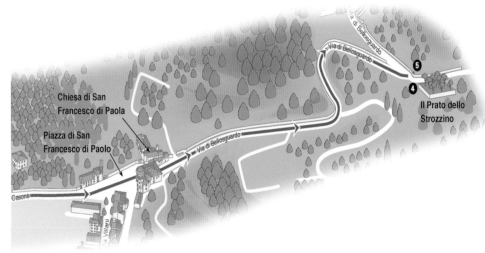

A Hill with a View: Bellosguardo

Villa Brichier Colombi.

6 Once you've taken a breather, continue up the sharp bend of **Via di Bellosguardo** until you reach the top of the hill where you will see two villas straight ahead. The one on your right (**Via di Bellosguardo, 20, Brichier Colombi**) was where Henry James vacationed. Whilst the closed-off courtyard and modest façade give little away, one can imagine him sitting on his balcony writing the *The Aspern Papers*, whilst taking inspiration from the view of the city you see on your left, which made a profound impression on him (see **Introduction**, page 17). Whilst this viewpoint is technically a foretaste of the showstopper in store, you can see where James was coming from.

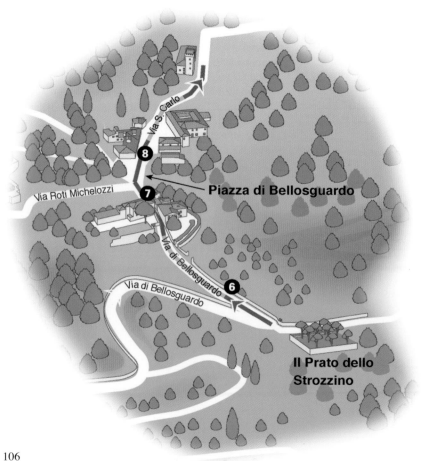

One of the tabernacles on Via di Bellosguardo.

7 Follow the paved path ahead between the two villas, and you emerge into **Piazza di Bellosguardo**. Walk straight ahead across this long *piazza*, past pretty villa gates weeping with wisteria (one of which was briefly the home of Galileo) and you will reach **Via San Carlo** at the opposite end.

8 Head up the narrow **Via San Carlo** and stop at the turreted tower, belonging to the medieval **Villa Montauto**. It was here Nathaniel Hawthorne (author of *The Scarlet Letter*) stayed for two months in 1858. Whilst he complains in his diary that the walk from Florence was 'hot and disagreeable' he was more than contented with the destination: 'I like my present residence immensely. The house stands on a hill overlooking Florence and is big enough to quarter a regiment...At one end of the house there is a moss-grown tower, haunted by owls and by the ghost of a monk' – the monk in question being no other than the fanatical 15thC theocrat, Savanorola. Hawthorne, like James, was so inspired by this spot that he resolved to 'take it away bodily and clap it into a Romance, which I have in my head ready to be written out.' On your right, a view of Florence's suburbs stretches out before you.

The view from Villa Montauto.

Above, heraldic eagle on the gate of a villa in Bellosguardo. Left, the view from the top of Via di Bellosguardo.

A Hill with a View: Bellosguardo

9 Retrace your steps to **Piazza di Bellosguardo**, turning right down **Via Roti Michelozzi** (just past the raised garden temple). This road leads to the gates of **Torre di Bellosguardo** – a frescoed medieval property, now the seat of a four-star hotel. Unfortunately the grounds are private, so take a peek into its gardens at your own risk. Besides, the real treat is the famous viewpoint positioned just before the hotel's gates, from which you can see the façades of every one of Florence's major churches (from left to right these are Santa Maria Novella, the Duomo, Santo Spirito and Santa Croce). Encapsulating Florentine history with heart-stopping intimacy, this view arguably rivals the more famous vista seen from

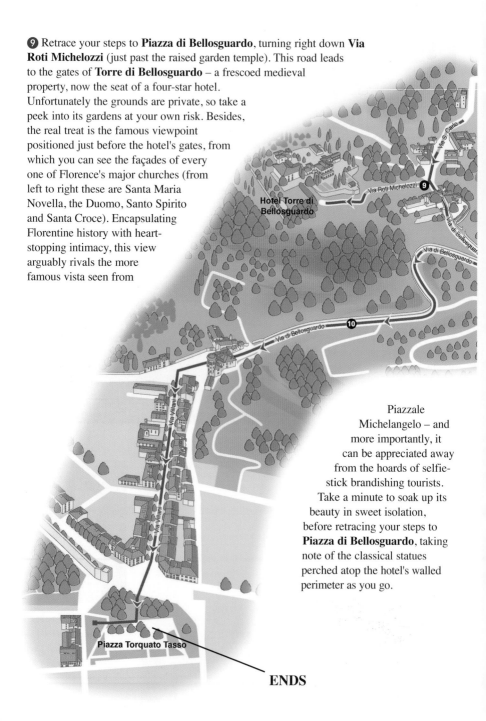

Piazzale Michelangelo – and more importantly, it can be appreciated away from the hoards of selfie-stick brandishing tourists. Take a minute to soak up its beauty in sweet isolation, before retracing your steps to **Piazza di Bellosguardo**, taking note of the classical statues perched atop the hotel's walled perimeter as you go.

ENDS

The famous view across Florence from Torre Bellosguardo.

🔟 Head all the way back down **Via di Bellosguardo**, gazing at the view through shifting light as the day wears on. Once you've reached **Piazza di San Francesco di Paolo**, instead of heading back down Via del Casone, take a left down **Via Villani**. This will take you straight to **Piazza Torquato Tasso** – the ideal spot to lunch/dine after your labours. The square is charmingly rough-and-tumble, and compared to its glitzier neighbour Santo Spirito it retains a distinctly authentic, local atmosphere – drawing in a trickle of colourful characters from surrounding squats. In spite of this it has a number of prime eateries lacing its right side, including **Culinaria** (a mix of Tuscan and Moroccan) or **Trattoria BBQ** catering to hardened carnivores. The star of the show however is **La Sorbettiera**, the little-known but exceptional *gelateria* – *Limone e Salvia* (lemon and sage) and *Caramello* are our two favourite flavours.

Above, villa gates. Below, wall of Torre di Bellosguardo.

Piazza Torquato Tasso.

Last Supper Trail

This scavenger hunt – to discover the most interesting and beautiful *Last Supper* paintings dotted about the city – is for art lovers, and for the curious. Florence's *cenacoli* (the refectories of monasteries, where *Last Suppers* are typically found) are easily the city's best-kept secrets, often free to visit and tucked away from the crowds. While the sheer volume of art in Florence can easily overwhelm any visitor trying to get to grips with the Florentine Renaissance, looking at this subject on its own provides a perfect window for understanding the seismic shift it represented. Our chosen *Last Suppers* span from the Gothic period to the beginning of Mannerism. Its changing iconography was the product of a small but forward-thinking city, in which artists bounced ideas off each other, and created trends that would spread their tentacles across Italy and the rest of Europe. Take Leonardo da Vinci's *Last Supper*,

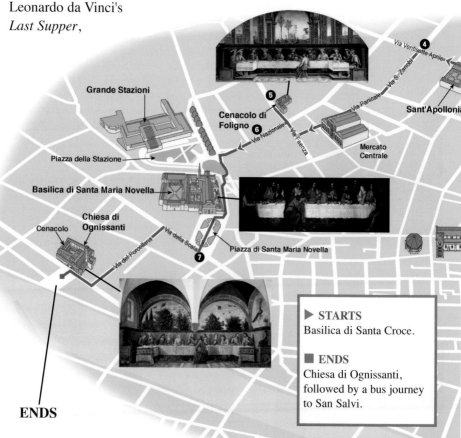

ENDS

> ▶ **STARTS**
> Basilica di Santa Croce.
>
> ■ **ENDS**
> Chiesa di Ognissanti, followed by a bus journey to San Salvi.

for example. One of the most iconic images in the world, it's often referred to as the first Renaissance *Last Supper*. What few people realize is that Florence was the 'Capital of *cenacoli*' long before Leonardo painted his masterpiece in Milan in 1494, and as a native Florentine he would have seen and been inspired by a number of *Last Suppers* on this trail.

Beginning at Santa Croce, where the first Florentine *Last Supper* was painted in 1350, the walk then boomerangs across central Florence, ending up at Chiesa di Ognissanti. After this we advise you to take a bus to San Michele a San Salvi, to look at Andrea del Sarto's *Last Supper* from 1525 – the *pièce de résistance* of the genre. All of the *Last Suppers* on this trail (except San Salvi) can be integrated into the other walks in this guide, so you may wish to skip those you've already seen. For example if you've completed **Walking With Ghosts**, pages 40-49, and paid entry to the Basilica di Santa Croce, feel free to adjust the starting point. The other *cenacoli* are all free to enter, and we think it's worth revisiting these sites to look at their *Last Suppers* alone. Start early, as the majority of *cenacoli* shut around lunchtime.

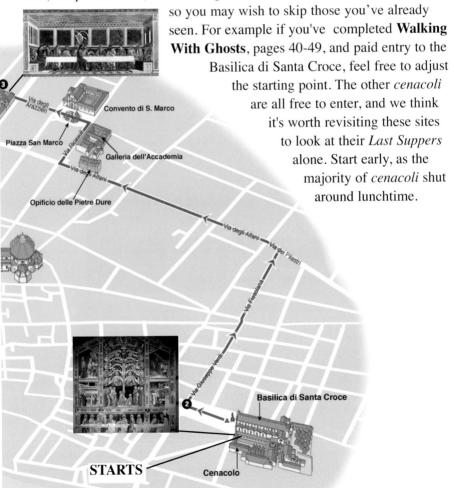

❶ Head to the refectory in the **Basilica di Santa Croce**, open Mon – Sat between 9.30am and 5.30pm (turn to pages 44-45 of **Walking With Ghosts** for commentary on the rest of the Basilica. If you've already done this walk and paid entry, feel free to make Sant'Apollonia your starting point). Here you'll find the first recorded Florentine *Last Supper*, painted by Taddeo Gaddi between 1335-50. An example of the Gothic style, it pre-dates the techniques of perspective and realism that would strike half a century later, but the

Basilica di Santa Croce.

wonderful wackiness of Gaddi's fresco has a magic all of its own. It's dominated by a giant *Crucifixion* with scrolls blossoming from it that bear prophecies of Christ's sacrifice, and protrude images of the prophets themselves, like baubles on a macabre Christmas tree.

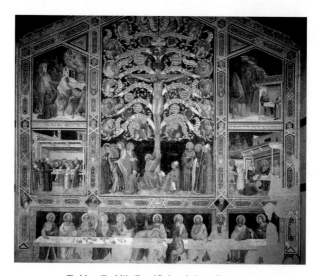

Taddeo Gaddi's Crucifixion & Last Supper.

The figures in his *Last Supper* are stiff and distorted, and in the typically literal language of Gothic art, Judas' diminutive size reflects his meagre morality. But in many ways this first *Last Supper* set a surprisingly resilient precedent: on this walk you'll repeatedly see apostles lined across a rectangular table, with a caricatured Judas singled out on the other side; you'll also see a number of sleeping St. Johns, a bizarre reflection of John as the 'contemplative' apostle. And finally, you'll see Jesus pointing at the cup of wine that Judas dips his bread in, reflecting both the moment Christ reveals Judas' betrayal (*'The one who has dipped his hand into the bowl with me will betray me'*) and Jesus' institution of the Eucharist, when the wine and bread turn into the blood and body of Christ. The complex dual narrative was exactly why artists found the *Last Supper* such a rich and beguiling subject.

❷ Leave the basilica and cross **Piazza Santa Croce**, turning right down **Via Giuseppe Verdi**, which will eventually merge into **Via Fiesolana**. After ten minutes you'll reach the end, and take a left down **Via dei Pilastri** – which soon merges on to **Via degli Alfani**. On your right, at **no. 78**, you'll pass the **Opificio delle Pietre Dure** – a museum and restoration centre founded in 1588 that celebrates the Florentine craft of inlaying gems and semi-precious stones to create images. Take a right at **Via Ricasoli**, which takes you past the **Galleria dell'Accademia** and into **Piazza San Marco**. Cross the *piazza* and go down **Via degli Arazzieri**.

Above, the Medici arms. Below, trellis roses. Both are pietra dura designs from the Opifico delle Pietre Dure.

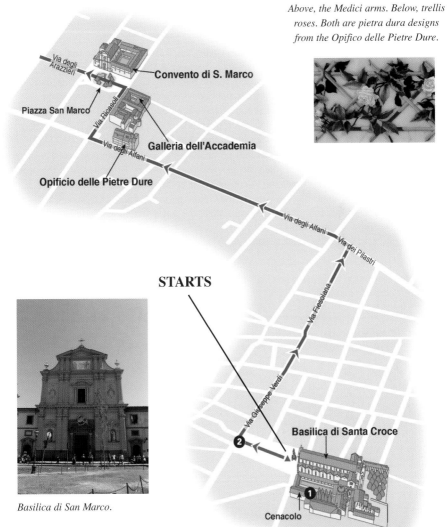

STARTS

Basilica di San Marco.

113

Andrea del Castagno's Last Supper.

❸ When the road merges on to **Via Ventisette Aprile**, you'll find the entrance to **Cenacolo di Sant'Apollonia** on your left at **no. 1**, open daily between 8.15am and 1.50pm (it also features in the walk, **Sacred Space**s, page 53). Inside the *cenacolo* of this small Benedictine nunnery is the *Last Supper* that changed it all, painted by Andrea del Castagno between 1445-50, and considered by those in-the-know to have been the first of the Renaissance. Finished exactly a century after Taddeo Gaddi's, the markers of a Renaissance style that had been gathering momentum since 1400 leap out at you. Firstly, the influence of Classicism: Castagno sets his scene in a Classical covered porch, in which sit the sculptural apostles in Grecian robes. Secondly, the use of linear perspective (developed by Brunelleschi at the turn of the century), which enables Castagno to construct his architectural space and draw the viewer in to this dimensional illusion. During the Gothic period, flatness in frescos was simply accepted as a limitation of the medium – this new way of painting would have had a novel magic for the viewing public.

Castagno's Judas.

Castagno's fresco is remarkable in a number of other ways. His colours and bold geometric patterns are as vibrant as ever, almost Byzantine in flavour. Particularly striking is the lightening bolt erupting from the psychedelic marble panel in the centre, to hail Judas as a traitor. One thread of continuity with Gaddi is the characteristic depiction of Judas, with dark hair, a sallow complexion and a hook nose – as well as a snoozing St. John on Jesus' left side.

❹ Take a look at the rest of the *cenacolo's* small but charming collection, before turning left outside **Sant'Apollonia**, continuing down **Via Ventisette Aprile**. After one block take a left down **Via S. Zanobi**. Continue as it merges onto **Via Panicale**, down the side of the **Mercato Centrale** (always a good gastronomic stop), eventually turning right down **Via Faenza**. On your right at **no. 40** you'll find **Cenacolo di Foligno** – a former convent of a Tertiary Franciscan order. As we went to press its opening hours were Tuesdays from 8.30am-12.30pm, and Wednesdays from

8.15am-13.50pm, but we advise you to check beforehand (it also features on **Power and Patronage**, page 34).

❺ Inside **Cenacolo di Foligno** is a *Last Supper* that was only rediscovered in the 19thC, and initially thought to be a lost Raphael. It's now believed to have been painted by Pietro Perugino between 1493-96 – almost exactly the same time that Leonardo was painting his famous Milanese version. Half a century on from Andrea del Castagno and a few more innovations have been thrown into the mix. First, the use of a U-shaped table, and the depiction of a landscape in the background – all methods of enhancing the illusion of depth. As you'll see later, these were first introduced by Ghirlandaio in 1480, though Perugino went a step further by depicting in the landscape the scene of an angel appearing before Jesus in the Garden of Gethsemane, to harden his resolve before the Crucifixion. By collapsing time he symbolically unites this scene with the Last Supper. An even more poignant innovation is his depiction of Judas, no longer Satyr-like, but an ordinary looking man. He holds 30 pieces of silver – his bribe money for betraying Jesus – and stares directly at the viewer, reeling us into his personal narrative. His gaze seems to hold the sum of human weakness, reminding the viewer how easy it is to fall into temptation.

Pietro Perugino's Last Supper.

115

6 The rest of the museum displays works by 16thC artists who were inspired by Perugino, and are worth looking at before leaving the *cenacolo* and turning left, then first right down **Via Nazionale**. Keep going until you emerge into **Piazza della Stazione**, home to Florence's Brutalist train station, and bear left down **Via degli Avelli**, along the side of the basilica, arriving into **Piazza di Santa Maria Novella**. As we went to press the **Basilica di Santa Maria Novella** was due to display, for the first time, Plautilla Nelli's *Last Supper*, after an extended period of restoration. Nelli was a self-taught nun painting in the 1570s, and a devotee of the teachings of the extremist monk Savonarola. Her *Last Supper* stands out from others on this trail for its use of oil-on-canvas, an exciting new medium introduced in the 16thC, which opened up the potential for expressing colour and light.

Basilica di Santa Maria Novella.

Today Nelli is lauded for the emotion and sentiment in her work, but perhaps most of all her *Last Supper* poses questions about gender – and how, when female painters were expected to stick to small devotional pieces, Nelli had the confidence to tackle a large-scale subject that put her on par with Florentine masters such as Leonardo da Vinci and Andrea del Sarto.

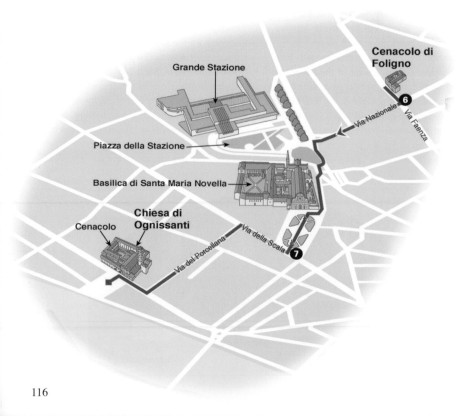

Plautilla Nelli's Last Supper.

7 Cross the **Piazza di Santa Maria Novella**, turning right at the end down **Via della Scala** and then left down **Via del Porcellana**. Go right down **Borgo Ognissanti** to reach **Piazza Ognissanti** with its *chiesa* of the same name. The *cenacolo* of Ognissanti's convent is located between its two cloisters, and open Mondays, Tuesdays and Saturdays between 9am-12pm (the Chiesa di Ognissanti also features on the walk **Power and Patronage**, page 37). Here you'll find Domenico Ghirlandaio's *Last Supper* fresco, painted in 1480. Although not widely known outside of Florence today, in many ways Ghirlandaio was the quintessential Renaissance painter of his day. He was almost fanatical about his use of perspective, using in this *Last Supper* real architectural features to enhance the illusions of a covered classical porch. He was also the first to suggest a landscape

Chiesa di Ognissanti.

beyond the scene itself. Ghirlandaio was master at rooting religious scenes to every day life: here, the tableware is rendered in precious detail, and the apostles are depicted without halos, lending an unusually secular note to the scene – the influence of Classical Humanism. But piety is there for those canny enough to decipher his symbolism. The ripe apricots denote sin, while the lettuce evokes penance; the ruby-red cherries foreshadow Christ's sacrifice, while the errant peacock, with its potential to spread its regal plumes, was a well-known symbol for his resurrection. The Renaissance, with all its cerebral underpinnings, was clearly well under way.

Left, Ghirlandaio's Last Supper. Below, close-up of his peacock, a symbol of Christ's resurrection.

San Michele a San Salvi.

❽ Once you've had your fill of *Last Suppers* in the inner city of Florence, it's time to make your way to **San Michele a San Salvi** on the outskirts of Florence, for the grand finale of the genre (this part of the walk does not feature on the map). The monastery is open Tuesday – Sunday, between 8.15am and 1.50pm. Whether you have time to squeeze this into your morning or wish to save it for another day, the museum is well worth the journey. Either catch the **No. 6** bus from **Piazza Adua**, next to **SMN Station**, or the **No. 6/No. 20** from **Piazza San Marco**. 30 or 17 minutes later (depending on where you leave from), get off at **Lungo L'Affrico** and head south on **Via Lungo L'Affrico**, taking the first left down **Via Tito Speri** to get to **San Michele a San Salvi** in **Piazza di San Salvi**.

Andrea del Sarto's dashing Judas.

❾ The remarkable museum of this Vallumbrosan monastery (which dates back to 1048) is free to wander, often in splendid isolation due to the slightly out-of-the-way location. Its undisputed masterpiece is Andrea del Sarto's *Last Supper* painted between 1520-25, found in the *cenacolo*. The 16thC chronicler Giorgio Vasari described this fresco as *his [del Sarto's] most spectacular masterpiece, and one of the most beautiful paintings in the world...it being so fine that whoever sees it is stupefied.* And he wasn't wrong. A mere four years after its completion, during the deadly siege of Florence when its suburbs were being destroyed, Charles V's troops allegedly saw this fresco and stopped dead in their tracks, refusing to put another stone of the monastery out of place.

So what had them so bowled over? The painting depicts a moment of intense, almost cinematic drama, focused on the revelation of Judas' betrayal. For the first time Judas sits at the side of Jesus, and points to himself incredulously, while several disciples stand up and point

The interior of San Salvi church.

at him in shock and horror. The notion of a 'moment in time' would later become paramount during the Baroque, making this painting especially unique and forward-thinking. The two figures on the upper-balcony – a servant and master – are akin to us, the audience: incidental intruders on this dramatic scene, which seems to be happening in-the-now, rather than belonging to a remote biblical past.

Above, Andrea del Sarto's Last Supper. *Below right, a detail.*

Known in his lifetime as an artist *senza errori* ('without error') del Sarto's *Last Supper* – painted on the cusp of Mannerism – is often considered to be the apogee of the achievements of the Florentine Renaissance. Comparing Taddeo Gaddi's esoteric and strange *Last Supper* to the realism and vivacity of Del Sarto's apostles, makes it clear how far artistic representation had come in the space of just under two centuries. There's no symbolism, and certainly no halos – the scene feels secular to the point of being modern – which is perhaps why Charles' army felt so overwhelmed in its presence.

Etruscan Delights: Fiesole

The story of Fiesole's origins remains elusive, bound up as it is with a mysterious people called the Etruscans. Making their way to Tuscany around 700BC – either by sea from the Balkans or by land from Asia Minor – the Etruscans were expert potters, metalworkers and merchants. They managed to expand their Empire as far as Rome before being defeated in 308BC, when Fiesole was assimilated into the Roman Empire. Its loss of independence heralded the town's gradual economic decline, at the same time when Florence – their much younger neighbour, who may also have been founded by the Etruscans – was in ascendance, finally managing to conquer Fiesole in 1125.

View of Piazza Mino, Fiesole's main piazza.

A day-trip to Fiesole (20 minutes by bus) should be high on any visitor's list. Whilst Florence is in many ways firmly planted in the 15thC, the multi-layered history of Fiesole is palpable at every turn. Excavations have uncovered remnants from the Neolithic period through to the town's Etruscan, Roman and Florentine occupations – exhibited throughout its ruins, monasteries and museums. Not to mention the near unparalleled beauty of its hillside location, which has kept Fiesole a popular outpost for Florentines during the hot summer months. This walk takes you on a tour of the town's attractions, before taking you down the Old Road of Fiesole to the sleepy hamlet of San Domenico, where you can catch a bus back to Florence.

Left, terracotta Christ child made by Giovanni della Robbia. Right, equestrian monument of Victor Emmanel II and Garibaldi

Archeological Site

Bandini
Museum

Convento di
San Francesco

Cattedrale di
San Romolo

Archeological
Museum

4

5

Town Hall

2 **3**

8

STARTS

7

6 **1**

9 Piazza Mino

Chiesa di
Santa Maria
Primerana

Via Vecchia Fiesolana

La Villa Medici
a Fiesole

Chiesa di Sant'Ansano

Via Vecchia Fiesolana

10 Via Bandini

Via Bandini

Via Vecchia Fiesolana

▶ **STARTS**
Piazza Mino. Bus stop:
Fiesole Piazza Mino

■ **ENDS**
Piazza San Domenico.
Bus stop: San
Domenico.

11

12 Via Della Badia die Roccetini

Convento di
San Domenico

Piazza San Domenico

ENDS

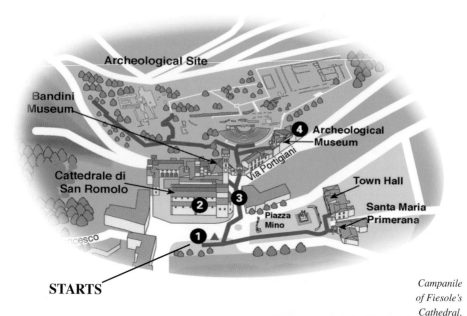

Archeological Site

Bandini Museum

4 Archeological Museum

Via Portigiani

Cattedrale di San Romolo

Town Hall

Santa Maria Primerana

2 **3**

Piazza Mino

ncesco

1 ▲

STARTS

Campanile of Fiesole's Cathedral.

1 Hop on the **No.7** bus in **Piazza San Marco**, which will take you up the winding road to Fiesole. After 20 or 30 minutes (depending on traffic) get off at **Piazza Mino**, Fiesole's main square, where there is often a market being held, including a particularly good antiques market every first Sunday of the month. Climb the steps behind the bronze equestrian statue, which depicts *Victor Emmanel II and Garibaldi*, two heroes of the *Risorgimento*. Go inside the benighted interior of **Santa Maria Primerana**, whose origins date back to the 10thC, where you can admire a terracotta *Crucifixion* at the altar by the Della Robbia workshop. To the left of the church is the city's town hall,

Il Verso del Tempo (The Arrow of Time) - by Antonio Crivelli.

embellished with the coats of arms of Fiesole's 16thC magistrates.

2 Head across the square to the 12thC **Cathedral**, dedicated to San Romolo – the first pastor of Fiesole to be appointed by St Peter, before he was martyred under Domitian, the Roman Emperor. The most impressive feature of the austere interior is its columns, a few of which are topped by original Roman capitals. Head to the right of the presbytery to find the marble monument of Bishop Leonardo Salutati, designed by Mino da Fiesole – the 15thC artist who gives his name to the town square.

❸ Outside of the cathedral turn left and left again in the direction of its honey-coloured *campanile*. Straight ahead will be the entrance to the **Archaeological Site and Museum** (**Via Portigiani**, **1**, open daily). Here the palimpsest of Fiesolian history is laid bare, showing remnants from its Etrusco-Roman past (there have even been traces from the Neolithic period found here, now in the Museum). The 3,000-seat **Teatro Romano** is its best preserved ruin, remarkably still used for open-air summer operas. Beyond this are the Roman Baths, followed the sparse remains of a Roman Temple. These conceal the even sparser remains of an Etruscan temple, which the Romans built upon when they conquered the city.

The Teatro Romano.

Ruins of Etrusco-Roman Temples.

Left, pietra dura ornament in Santa Maria Primerana church.
Right, a Roman bust in the Archaeologial Museum.

❹ The **Archaeological Museum** exhibits artefacts found on the site as well as in the surrounding hills – a melange of Etrusco-Roman tombs, statues and artefacts, curated to tell the story of Fiesole's ancient history and the various excavations that have uncovered it. Pottery enthusiasts should head upstairs to see the Constantine collection, displaying Corinthian, Attic and Etruscan vases.

Etruscan Delights: Fiesole

5 Leave the site and the **Bandini Museum** will be on your right (**Via Portigiani, 1**). The former collection of the 18thC cleric, Angelo Bandini, is small but precious, its well-chosen pieces succinctly telling the story of Tuscan art from the medieval period to the High Renaissance. A ground-floor room is devoted to works by the Della Robbia workshop, recognisable for their blue-and-white terracotta sculptures.

The Visitation, made by Giovanni della Robbia, in the Bandini Museum.

6 Back at **Piazza Mino** have a *caffè* and panini at **Cafe Deja Vu** before heading up **Via San Francesco**, a narrow stone-paved road that climbs 200 metres up the **Hill of St Francis**. After about 50 m, you will pass the entrance to **The Memorial Garden**, containing two monuments: one dedicated to citizens of Fiesole who died in the First World War; the other to *carabiniere* killed by the Nazis in the Second World War. On your right at **no. 18** is **La Reggia**, ideal for a romantic dinner with views.

The view from Convento di San Francesco.

7 A little further along you come to a level spot known both as *la banchina* due to the small bench, and *belvedere*, due to the splendid view it offers of Florence and the surrounding valley. Pause here before continuing to the top of the hill, where the **Convento di San Francesco** is perched. This was once quaintly named 'St Mary of the Flowers', and was formerly the abode of a group of women called 'The Recluses of Alexander'. The Franciscans took over in 1399. The church's great masterpiece is *The Immaculate Conception*, attributed to the 15thC eccentric Piero di Cosimo, who was known for shrugging off prevailing Renaissance influences in favour of a more whimsical, Netherlandish style. The 16thC chronicler Giorgio Vasari claimed the artist was pathologically terrified of fire and lived off nothing but boiled eggs. Amongst other things the convent has a museum exhibiting yet more Etrusco-Roman and Egyptian artefacts.

Above, the view from la banchina, on the Hill of St Francis. Right, Madonna and Child in the Bandini Museum.

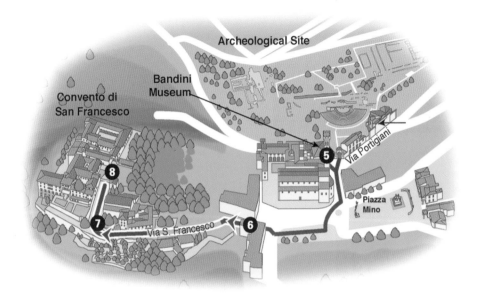

8 Nip into the charming gift shop before retracing your steps down **Via San Francesco** (or alternatively going through the iron gate in this courtyard which also merges back onto this road), making your way back to **Piazza Mino**.

Left going clockwise: terracotta angel by Giovanni della Robbia; the inner courtyard of Convento di San Francesco; the exterior of Convento di San Francesco; the convent's outer courtyard.

125

Top, the view from Via Vecchia Fiesolana. Above, the Chiesa Sant'Ansano.

9 Turn right down the main road on the square's corner. Don't follow it round, but head straight down the walled, leafy path of **Via Vecchia Fiesolana**, which until 1840 was the only road to Fiesole. This charming walkway runs through olive groves, linden trees and cypresses, played out to the croak of cicadas, with a view of Florence stretching out below. Soon on your right you'll pass **Villa Medici Fiesole**, its elegant loggia glimpsable from over its garden wall. This was commissioned from Michelozzo by Cosimo the Elder, and inherited by his son Lorenzo Il Magnifico who turned it into a gathering place for artists, philosophers and intellectuals.

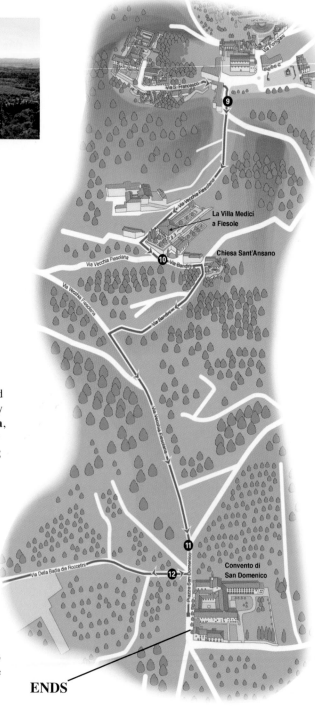

La Villa Medici a Fiesole

Chiesa Sant'Ansano

Convento di San Domenico

ENDS

⑩ When the road forks do not follow the bend right, instead keep straight on what is now **Via Bandini**. At the end of the road you'll see the small yellow façade of **Chiesa di Sant'Ansano**, constructed in the 12thC. Turn right, continuing along **Via Bandini**, and you will ultimately rejoin **Via Vecchia Fiesolana**, where you turn left. On your right at **no. 62** will appear the *Riposo dei Vescovi* (Bishops Rest) so-called for being a resting place for clergymen travelling from Florence by foot or horse.

The view from Villa Medici Fiesole.

⑪ Emerge into **Piazza San Domenico**, with the **Convento di San Domenico** on its left side, residence of the beatific monk Fra Angelico until 1436, when he moved to San Marco. Inside is his *Madonna Enthroned*, also known as 'The Fiesole Altarpiece.' Take a seat on one of the wooden pews to appreciate the *tromp l'oeil* ceiling fresco, which vividly depicts the Madonna ascending to heaven with a host of angels.

⑫ To complete your tour of San Domenico head down **Via Della Badia dei Roccettini**, directly opposite the church entrance to get to **Badia Fiesolana** (just out of range of our map). This was formerly the Cathedral of Fiesole until 1028 when it was transformed into a Benedictine Abbey (it is now the seat of the European University). You cannot go inside, but you can admire its inlaid Prato marble façade framed by rusticated stone – a strange combination of Santa Maria Novella and San Lorenzo in one. Finally, return to **Piazza San Domenico** where you can catch the **No.7** bus back to **Piazza San Marco** in Florence.

Far left, Badia Fiesolana.
Left, the Convento di San Domenico.

Ella Carr read English at Edinburgh University, and is currently working as a travel guide editor and writer. She has a special interest in Florence, where she spent several weeks researching for this guide.